With best wishes

Andrew C Ferguson

LEGACY OF THE SACRED CHALICE

A SECRET VISION BECOMES A (MODERN) RITUAL

Lodge No. 0, Kilwinning

The current headquarters of Kilwinning Lodge, reputedly the oldest Masonic Lodge in the world, stands in the shadow of Kilwinning Abbey in Ayrshire, Scotland.

LEGACY OF THE SACRED CHALICE

A SECRET VISION BECOMES A (MODERN) RITUAL

BY

C. BRUCE HUNTER
ANDREW C. FERGUSON

ILLUSTRATIONS BY ALISON FERGUSON

Macoy Publishing & Masonic Supply Co., Inc.
Richmond, Virginia

Copyright, 2001

C. Bruce Hunter
AND
Andrew C. Ferguson
Chapel Hill, North Carolina

Published by
Macoy Publishing & Masonic Supply Co., Inc.
Richmond, Virginia

ISBN - 0-88053-091-X

Printed In the United States of America

TABLE OF CONTENTS

Portions of this book have been drawn from the following articles:

"THE ROLE OF THE ROYAL ORDER OF SCOTLAND IN THE SCISM OF 1751 AND THE UNION OF 1813." Ars Quatuor Coronatorum, vol 109, 1997.

"THE GRAIL AND THE LODGE – MASONIC ANTECED-ENTS IN THE 12TH CENTURY." Ars Quatuor Coronatorum, vol 112, 2000.

INTRODUCTION

When, where and why was the Masonic ritual created? This question has plagued historians for centuries. It is in fact one of the Fraternity's most mystifying enigmas, and the members themselves are the main reason it remains unresolved.

Part of the reason is easy to understand. Although Masons insist that they are not a secret society, they freely admit that they are a "society with secrets," and as such they have always tried to protect anything they consider suitable for members only. As a result, they talk little and commit even less to paper. So it is not surprising that the history of their ritual - perhaps the most secret part of the whole organization – is not as well documented as it should be. But there is more to it than that.

Before the Grand Lodges arose in the 1700's, Masonry was a loose alliance of individual lodges. They often kept poor records, and few of them felt the need to maintain a detailed account of their history. From what we understand of those days, Freemasonry was once a craft organization dedicated to supporting the workers who built the gothic cathedrals. They probably thought that no one, including their own future members, would be interested in their daily activities. Consequently, they did little in the way of record keeping.

Then there was the inevitable loss of records. It is the bane of an old organization that many of its documents are destroyed over the years. Fire, flood and decay have all played their part in the destruction of papers that were meant to be kept for posterity. Especially in the late Middle Ages, when the standard filing system consisted of tossing loose pieces of paper onto a dusty shelf, even important documents had little chance of surviving through several **centuries.**

And finally there was the problem of widespread illiteracy. Until fairly recent times, most people had little need to read and write. So the modern penchant for keeping records was virtually unknown. Maintaining a library – much less an archive – was an activity limited to a few monks, scholars and noblemen, and even then it was only a part time activity.

In practical terms, this means that if we're interested in the history of the masonic ritual, we can trace it back about three centuries. That's as far as surviving documents will take us. We can only speculate about the form the ritual might have had in earlier days.

Of course, rituals used during the twentieth century are easy to research. Members of the Craft have access to them, and non-members who go to the trouble soon discover that they are not impossible to locate. After a few inquiries in the right places, anyone can obtain a reasonably factual copy of the modern ritual from a used book store.

We also know what the ritual was like during the 1800's, because by that time records were finally being kept on a regular basis and we actually have copies of them. Some are fakes, of course, and it is often hard to sort out which copies are authentic, but at least we have something to go on.

The 1700's are a little more difficult. Several copies of the ritual have survived from that century, but we have little information about them. Most are what historians call "exposed" rituals. They were published unofficially, often by avowed enemies of Freemasonry who were not at all interested in providing an unbiased picture of the Fraternity.

Apparently some of these exposes are accurate versions of Masonic procedures as they existed then. But others are full of errors. And to the practiced eye it is obvious that a few are completely fictitious. At best, these documents are difficult to authenticate. At worst, they are little more than the fantasies of people who had probably never seen a real Masonic ritual or attended a lodge meeting.

While this can be something of a nuisance to the casual reader, it poses a serious problem for historians. With so little information available, it is difficult to know what to do with these rituals. We simply aren't sure which if the exposes are accurate and which are fakes with little or no similarity to the real thing.

Ordinarily we could look farther back in history to find additional evidence. But in this case the earlier history of the Fraternity is no help at all. The 1600's are an extremely poor source of information about the Masons. We have virtually no official documents from that era, and since everyone agrees that the ritual went through significant changes during the 1700's, we can only wonder what it was like *before* the changes occurred. So the material it may have contained a century earlier is anyone's guess.

And before the 1600's? Historians aren't even sure there was a ritual at that time. If there was, it was probably a very simple initiation ceremony, consisting of little more than welcoming the new member to the lodge and telling him its rules.

In addition, Masonry wasn't even a social fraternity as it is today. The traditional history of the organization claims that the modern "Craft" of Freemasonry evolved from the stone masons who built the gothic cathedrals of Europe and Britain, which means that it was originally a craft guild of sorts. It didn't become a social club until the construction of cathedrals died out in the sixteenth century and the lodges began accepting honorary members to keep themselves going.

Of course, nothing about Masonic history is simple. Even the theory we've just described is difficult to document. With only a few records available, there is plenty of room for speculation, and not everyone agrees that this is the way Freemasonry evolved. Although a "craft" origin was once the prevailing view, in recent years it has become fashionable to question whether the modern lodge had anything to do with medieval stone masons, and a number of other theories have been proposed to explain where it did come from.

These problems only complicate our search for the beginnings of the ritual, because they make us question our sources. Now we aren't even sure where to look for evidence. Many writers claim that the medieval Knights Templar hold the key. Others say it was a group of monks who went underground when Henry VIII cracked down on the Catholic Church in England. Still others believe a group of gentlemen created their own social club in the eighteenth century by simply borrowing the stone masons' traditions without having any actual ties with them. And these are only a few of the theories. They go on and on.

What this jumble of theories does to our quest is obvious. If we aren't sure what medieval organization the Masons evolved from, we can't know where to look for the Fraternity's earliest ritual. And if we are lucky enough to find that ritual, we might fail to recognize it.

Obviously at this late date it is extremely difficult to prove anything about the first Masonic ritual. There is hope, though. Clues are there for anyone who really wants to find them. Admittedly, they are hard to recognize and even harder to interpret. But following them leads to some surprising conclusions.

This book is the result of following those clues. It is the product of an investigation that has lasted more than thirty years and included more than a little luck along the way. Its authors started with a few enticing bits of evidence that the evolution of Freemasonry didn't happen precisely as it is described in the history books. That evidence, though sketchy, led to signs that the origins of the Masonic lodge were deliberately covered up. They fell victim to the intrigue and secrecy that marked one of the most violent periods of history. And by the time the need for secrecy had fallen away, the true story was so well hidden that it has remained a mystery ever since.

The following chapters present a detective story of sorts. It begins with a look at the eighteenth century, the earliest period from which we have reliable information about the Masons. In that century we discover that the Fraternity was embroiled in a series of disputes and, curiously, that those disputes revolved around the ritual. Nor were these disputes a trivial matter. They actually led to a breakup of the world's most important Masonic body, London's Premier Grand Lodge.

The way that commotion began and ended holds valuable clues to what the Freemasons were arguing about. Those clues, in turn, lead to another conflict, one which reaches well back into the Middle Ages. It was a time when Freemasonry as we know it today did not exist. But its forerunner was there – a secretive organization that hid in the rolling hills of Scotland and covered its tracks so well that most historians refuse to believe it ever existed.

The procedures used by this Scottish organization provided the basis for the modern Masonic ritual, but those procedures were not created in Scotland. They were based on an even older tradition, a tradition that seamlessly blended truth and fiction in what some believe was the most profound story ever written.

Although the tradition adopted by the Scottish secret society was already old when the Scots inherited it, even it was not the source of original Masonic ritual. It was the result of more than a century of secrecy and intrigue that grew from the tortured history of one of the most curious organizations that ever existed.

The real origin of the Masonic ritual is tied to *that* organization. It lies even deeper in the Middle Ages, on another continent and in a world where a story told in a royal court launched the most sublime quest the human mind could imagine – a quest that created a truly timeless ritual.

But to understand how all of this fits together, we will have to tell the story from the beginning. And our story begins in England, a country long seen as the cradle of Freemasonry.

CHAPTER 1

THE GRAND LODGE AND THE RITUAL

Echoes of History

OUR search for the very first Masonic ritual has to start somewhere, and the most logical place to start is in the Goose and Gridiron Tavern in London. That's where the Grand Lodge of England began its long and distinguished life and it's where, to make a long story short, the modern Masonic lodge was created.

The Grand Lodge of England was formed on June 24, 1717 and it was truly a watershed event in Masonic history. Everything that has ever happened to the Craft can be divided into the time before and the time after that one particular day.

This is not simply because a new organization had come into being. It goes much deeper. The beginning of what is called "the Grand Lodge era" marks a period of change that altered the nature of Freemasonry at its most basic level. What was once a fairly simple organization of craftsmen became a social and philosophical club. A small core of symbols was transformed into an elaborate system of moral instruction. And what must have started as a simple oath of secrecy turned into a preoccupation that has virtually dominated the Fraternity ever since.

And that, in a nutshell, was the genesis of most of the Fraternity's problems, not to mention the problems we will face as we search its history. A preoccupation with secrecy has vexed Freemasonry from the very beginning. Not only has it been the source of a great deal of criticism, but it

1

has also placed barriers in the way of anyone – Mason or non-Mason – who wants to understand what the commotion is all about.

When a man joins the organization, he is told that he must at all cost keep his new Fraternity's secrets. In fact, he is asked to take a solemn oath to do so. But he is not told precisely what the secrets are, either on this occasion or at any time in the future.

As a result, even the most active Masons find themselves in something of a quandary. They spend the rest of their lives believing they are under a strict obligation to keep secrets without knowing what those secrets are.

The new member may want to know the exact limits of this "Masonic" secrecy. But how is he to find out? His initiation leaves him in the dark. He doesn't know where to look for books on the subject. And although he probably receives a newsletter with his membership, it isn't much help.

It is true that the Craft's newsletters occasionally publish dialogs on the issue. Interested members submit letters to the editor asking how much they are allowed to discuss with their non-Masonic friends, and "experts" on the ritual make awkward attempts to provide answers. But it soon becomes obvious that even the experts know very little about the subject, so the question is never quite resolved.

The reason for this lack of progress is not hard to understand: the very secrecy that creates the problem keeps it from being solved. Since virtually all Masons are convinced their organization is steeped in secrecy, they are reluctant even to ask questions. Most believe it is somehow improper to delve into the subject – a misconception we will soon encounter again in a different context – and many think the answers to their questions don't even exist. They *assume* it would be futile to ask questions to which, again, they only *assume* no one knows the answers. So for most Masons the process of discovering the "what" and "why" of their lodge's secrecy never even gets started.

The result is a problem that perpetuates itself. Although everyone who encounters the lodge is curious about its inner workings, no one seems to know very much. Since no one knows very much, answers are quite scarce. And since answers are scarce, it is virtually impossible to learn about the organization. In short, there is a pervasive lack of knowledge that keeps everyone from gaining more knowledge.

Nor is this a recent problem. It has existed from the beginning of the Grand Lodge period – and even before. There are indications that from the earliest of times the Masons have had only a sketchy understanding of their own organization.

Perhaps we shouldn't find this surprising, given what we have just said about the quandary caused by the Craft's approach to secrecy. There's no reason to believe that the Masons of a few centuries ago were any better at dealing with the problem than today's Masons. But during the Craft's formative years, it was a different kind of problem. Back then, the members were not just trying to understand their organization. They were trying to build it into something new and different.

A New and Troubled Beginning

The members of the early Grand Lodge were putting together an organization that was already facing challenges which hadn't even existed a century earlier. They had something to work with – the bear bones of an older, more medieval society – but it needed a lot of changes to get it ready for the future. That's why the Grand Lodge was founded in the first place, to reshape the old "craft" into a modern organization. It's also why the Grand Lodge ran into trouble almost immediately.

For some reason, the Masonic lodge of the eighteenth century came complete with a peculiar brand of secrecy. It was apparently very similar to the secrecy the lodge has today, but it had a more profound effect on what the Masons of *that* day were trying to accomplish. When they set out to reshape the old craft, they found themselves in the dark about a wide range of topics. They didn't know exactly what they were dealing with. And what they didn't know really did hurt them.

Their first tentative steps seem to have been more than a little confused. They apparently blundered into a serious dispute right away, creating problems that took almost a century to resolve. And they left records so sketchy that even historians who study the period have a hard time figuring out what was going on.

In particular, the years just before 1717 are a problem for anyone who wants to understand the history of Freemasonry and the dispute that almost tore it apart. The late 1600's and early 1700's were when the Masons decided to revamp their organization, and historians would love to know what the old organization was like, but unfortunately the information isn't there. The Fraternity's symbolism and ritual do imply that the modern lodge evolved from the medieval stone masons, though it has always been difficult to prove the two were ever connected.

The old craft of stone masonry is certainly a fitting heritage for modern Masons to claim. During the Middle Ages, the main source of employment for masons was in the field of ecclesiastical architecture – cathedrals, churches and an occasional private chapel commissioned and built by the very rich.

People familiar with modern architecture will appreciate the work required to build those medieval churches, but they may overlook the social status of the people who built them.

The religious structures of the day weren't merely places for holding meetings, and the people who made them weren't common laborers. Churches and chapels were ornately decorated with religious symbols, providing a visual means of teaching spiritual lessons. In a time when most people had no formal education and few skills, anyone who could fashion such marvelous things stood head and shoulders above the general population. The "mason" was therefore a highly skilled professional who turned raw stone into the most beautiful and sublime objects ever created, while his work brought him in contact with the leaders of the church, who in turn were only a step away from heaven.

In a way, the medieval mason was not far removed from the churchman. As a skilled craftsman, a mason had trade secrets that separated him from the rest of society. He spent most of his time dealing with religious subjects, even if he was merely carving them in stone and not preaching them from the pulpit. And he probably had a closely guarded password to prove to other members of the profession that he was part of their very select group.

But as time went on, things began to change. The Reformation ushered in a demand for simpler forms of worship. Ornate cathedrals, which were now in plentiful supply anyway, became less fashionable and no one felt the need to build new ones. As the last of them were finished – or nearly finished, since cathedrals always seem to need one more round of work – the masons had to turn their attention to secular buildings. And secular buildings have no need of religious symbols carved on their walls.

This was certainly a blow to the highly specialized craftsmen. After centuries as respected members of a lofty profession, they found their work less and less in demand.

The rise of learning that occurred near the end of the Middle Ages inflicted another blow to the craft of masonry. The individual craftsman, as skilled as he might be, was gradually replaced by methods influenced by the industrial model of doing things. Putting up a building no longer relied on the mysterious skill of a few. Plans were sketched almost casually by draftsmen, and the construction was done by contractors who moved routinely from job to job.

The talented artisan who was once educated in a monastery found himself replaced by a technician trained in a trade school. Brick and steel replaced stone as the preferred medium. Then standardized blueprints replaced the oral instructions and steady hand of the master architect who drew his plans one at a time.

But it wasn't just the business of putting up buildings that was changing. The organization which supported the stone mason had to change, too.

In the days of the gothic cathedral, the masons maintained something of a traveling lodge. The concept may seem out of date now, but at the time it was precisely what was needed. There weren't enough local craftsmen to erect a major building, so teams of architects and stone cutters were imported, often from long distances and occasionally from other countries. They did the job at hand, and when it was finished, or when individual craftsmen began to feel they had stayed in one place too long, they simply moved on to the next project.

Still, these craftsmen, like their modern counterparts, required an organization to take care of their needs and oversee their affairs. The solution was to set up a kind of "guild." It wasn't precisely the same as the trade guilds that were so common in medieval society. Those guilds organized and trained the local craftsmen who worked in a particular trade, and the masons were not local craftsmen. They were strangers who had traveled long distances to get to the job. (In fact, to this day a Freemason is sometimes called a "traveling man.") While they worked on a project, they needed a place to stay and facilities to prepare food. And they needed a support group to help them get along in a new place.

So the Masonic lodge evolved as an organization that was a little different from the local guild. It served many of the same functions, but it had the additional responsibility of tending to the needs of its rather unusual membership. In fact, the very word "lodge" implies that the meeting place was not a guild hall where locals came for occasional meetings, but was actually a place where traveling men could sleep and eat as well as tending to professional matters.

And since masons often traveled from one construction site to another, their lodges were not focused on strictly local affairs, as the craft guilds were. They had to keep an eye on what was happening at the cathedral that was being built several towns away. So they occasionally held assemblies to coordinate their affairs on a regional basis.

But as the era of gothic architecture came to a close and fewer and fewer ecclesiastical projects were launched, the need for *ad hoc* lodges and assemblies began to wane. The masons' lodge became more like the local craft guilds which had long been in business to support the other professions, and the masons themselves became more like their counterparts in the other crafts. They no longer traveled to the site of a cathedral or chapel. They now built the new town hall and the manor house and the Presbyterian church down the road.

The masons' lodge was gradually becoming a relic of an older age. During the fifteenth and sixteenth centuries, it became less relevant to both the society and the economy. What's more, the process obviously wasn't going to turn around, so it became increasingly apparent that the lodge had to change if it wanted to survive.

A Basis for Change

The lodge did have some things going for it. It had always performed a social function, seeing as it did to the needs of its members. And it had developed something of a mystique as a fellowship of elite artisans whose skills and work brought them close to the sublime. Now it took advantage of those strengths by inviting honorary members to join and by gradually evolving into a social club.

In short, the lodge capitalized on its good reputation in the community at a time when the community was ready for something new. As the Middle Ages came to a close, the world outside the lodge was changing, too. And a market was opening up for just what the lodge had to offer. So at precisely the right time, the masons got a much needed boost from the tide of history.

The closed world of the Middle Ages slowly gave way to a culture in which more and more people were becoming affluent and educated. Most of them were not aristocrats, and in the rigid class structure of the day, that meant they wouldn't be accepted into the higher strata of "polite" society. But they very much wanted some of the advantages of polite society. And at this very moment the Masonic lodge, which already had a built in measure of status, began widening its horizons by accepting new members.

The lodges now attracted wealthy merchants and businessmen by offering them an ancient heritage, a body of symbols and even an air of secrecy that was left over from the trade secrets and password of the medieval stone cutter. As the seventeenth century wore on, they did less building and more socializing. And as the European Enlightenment loomed on the horizon, their appeal as a fraternal organization finally overcame what little need they still had to function as a craft guild.

From this point on, secrecy and symbolism were among the lodge's most important features. Where masons once came together as a group to satisfy their needs as traveling craftsmen in want of food, shelter and professional support, they now came together as a fraternal group. No longer a practical organization, the lodge was merely an occasion for its members to get away from home for an evening of eating, drinking, socializing and philosophizing.

The masons were not the only such club. By the end of the seventeenth century, others existed as well. The various craft guilds had their own traditions to promote and many were evolving into social groups, while remnants of such outdated military units as the Royal Company of Archers were providing an outlet for men's chivalric fantasies. But the masons seemed to have the best mix of tradition and ceremony, so they were on their way to becoming the premier Fraternity of the British Isles, and eventually the world as well.

It is worth noting that historians distinguish the original lodge from the social club it became by capitalizing key words that refer to the new, social version of the organization. So "masons" were now "Masons," and the "craft" became the "Craft." But the lodge's evolution was not as sudden as this change in grammar might suggest. For many years groups of working, or "operative" stone masons attended lodge side by side with social, or "speculative" members.

Some lodges remained mostly operative for decades, while others were primarily speculative. However, the craft had clearly entered a period of transition, and at some point it must have become obvious to its members that it was slowly becoming a purely social organization.

The Need for a Grand Lodge

Of course, all transitions have their complications, and this one was no exception. The new "Masons" found that they had a significant hurdle to overcome. Masonic lodges had once been a loosely organized but international body. This was the form the craft needed to take in dealing with such massive projects as building the gothic cathedrals. Then as those major projects declined, the lodges became more local and even more loosely organized, if they could be described as organized at all. Now, as a budding social fraternity with units throughout Britain, the lodges felt the need for a greater degree of organization.

All of this came to a head on the evening of June 24, 1717 at the Goose and Gridiron Tavern in London. The tavern was a popular watering hole that stood near the spot where the modern offices of the Grand Lodge of England are now located on Great Queen Street. The Goose and Gridiron was where one of London's Masonic lodges held regular meetings, and since that particular lodge was the oldest, it seems to have been chosen to host a meeting of representatives from four of the city's lodges. The purpose of the meeting was to organize a ruling body to oversee their affairs.

All indications are that the members of these lodges weren't sure what they were trying to accomplish. In the early stages, they didn't keep good records. Or if they did keep records, they didn't do a good job of saving them, because virtually nothing has survived.

In addition, the operation seems to have gotten off to a slow start. It took years, not months, for them to write a constitution to define what they were doing. Even then, they seemed to move almost haphazardly to reshape a venerable organization into one designed to serve a new purpose. But

9

perhaps that is the way it has to be when a small group tries to build – or rebuild – something of importance.

In any event, the four lodges who came together that night to create a new Grand Lodge were a curious mix. In those days lodges did not have names as they do now. If anything, they were known by the taverns where they held their meetings.

These four lodges held their meetings at the Goose and Gridiron Alehouse, or Tavern (located in St. Paul's Churchyard), the Crown Alehouse (in Parker's Lane), the Apple Tree Tavern (in Charles Street), and the Rummer and Grapes Tavern (in Channel Row, Westminster).

The first of these lodges was supposedly established in 1691, though there is evidence that it was in existence a few decades earlier. It was operative and its members presumably worked on St. Paul's Cathedral during the last quarter of the seventeenth century. This lodge is now known as Antiquity Lodge No. 2. (It is traditional in Masonic circles for the oldest lodges to be assigned the lowest numbers, and how this lodge finally arrived in second place is relevant to our quest. But we will get around to that story a little later.)

The second lodge claimed to have been established in 1712. It was ill fated and seems to have gone out of business some time between 1736 and 1738.

The third was apparently very old. It was designated "time immemorial," which in Masonic jargon means that it has existed longer than anyone can remember. It later merged with another group called Cumberland Lodge and is now known as Fortitude and Old Cumberland Lodge No. 11.

The fourth was larger than the others and had attracted quite an array of aristocratic members. It originally met at the Rummer and Grapes Tavern but moved in about 1723 to the Horn Tavern in Palace Yard and was subsequently known as Horn Lodge. In 1774 it merged with Somerset House

10

Lodge and is now known as Royal Somerset House and Inverness Lodge No. 4.

By 1716, these four lodges had decided that they needed to organize their affairs a little better, and they called a meeting to decide how to proceed. Representatives gathered at the Apple Tree Tavern on Charles Street in Covent Garden and laid the foundation for the project, but even at this point the details are sketchy. One source says that the lodges met on St. John's Day but doesn't specify which of the two days that went by the same name. St John the Baptist's Day was on June 24, and St John the Evangelist's Day was December 27. Both have meaning for Masons, so the date of the meeting isn't certain.

What is certain is that during the evening the four lodges decided to form a Grand Lodge. In fact, they went so far as to designate themselves a Grand Lodge *pro tempore* ("for the time being"). Over the next few months, they did whatever groundwork was necessary. We aren't sure what that amounted to, because no records were left. But when all the preparations were completed, representatives of the four lodges convened again in the Goose and Gridiron and gave their seal of approval to the new Grand Lodge. A man named Anthony Sayer was elected and installed as its Grand Master, and the world's first Masonic Grand Lodge was off and running.

Toward a New Constitution

By all accounts, the Grand Lodge made reasonable progress during its early period. Within a few years it had grown to a dozen lodges, and in two decades it had more than a hundred. But from the outset there was still something that needed doing.

For centuries Masonic lodges had preserved and revered a document called the *Old* or *Gothic Constitutions* (sometimes called the *Old Charges*), which claimed to tell the story of the origins of English masonry. The document originated during the fourteenth century. It was copied and recopied until, by the eighteenth century, it existed in several versions. And it seems that the Grand Lodge wasn't satisfied with any of them. So in September of 1721 it appointed the Reverend Doctor James Anderson to prepare a "digest," which it could then use as its official constitution.

It isn't clear whether this was the Grand Lodge's idea or Anderson's. Some scholars think the good doctor, who was already a published author, jumped at an opportunity to profit from writing another book. He does seem to have made money on the deal, but whoever proposed it, the book has proved a boon for historians because the first and second editions of Anderson's *Constitutions* provide almost all the information we have about the first years of the Grand Lodge era.

Once he received his assignment, Anderson worked quickly. In December of 1721 – only three months after he got the job – the Grand Lodge appointed a committee of fourteen members to evaluate his finished manuscript. They made a few changes and reported their approval in March of the following year. And on January 17, 1723 Dr. Anderson presented a printed copy to the Grand Lodge at their quarterly meeting.

Anderson's *Constitutions* was now the official book of the Grand Lodge of England. It was printed and sold to anyone who wanted a copy. And it was later revised and reprinted as a second edition, which appeared in 1738.

But that isn't the whole story. If Anderson was the first to suggest a revision of the *Old Constitutions*, he may have been motivated by more than a desire to turn a profit. There is reason to believe he was one of a small group of men who brought an agenda with them when they became involved in the new Grand Lodge's affairs.

The Hidden Agenda

To understand the role this group may have played in the evolution of modern Freemasonry, we need to take a closer look at Anderson the man. And fortunately we have just enough information about him to make sense of his Masonic activities.

James Anderson lived from 1684 until 1739. Consequently, he was an eyewitness to the events leading up to the formation of the Grand Lodge as well as its early years of operation. More than that, he came from a Masonic family. He was the second son of a Scottish "Glassier and Measson" named James Anderson.

The older James was a member of Aberdeen Lodge, which met in the Scottish town of the same name, a hundred and fifty miles north of Edinburgh. He served as the lodge's secretary and as its master in 1688. (Some Masonic historians believe that the older James brought his son into the lodge during his term as master, but while we know that the younger James did become a Mason, the date of his initiation has since been lost.)

The younger James attended Marischal College in Aberdeen and became a minister in the Church of Scotland some time around 1702. He moved to London in 1707 but was back in Scotland in 1731 to receive the degree of Doctor of Divinity from Aberdeen University.

It was with this background that James Anderson made the *Old Constitutions* an integral part of Freemasonry at the precise moment the organization entered its modern period. But if he really was in it for more than the money, what interest could he have had in imposing this particular document on the Grand Lodge?

The answer to that question is the key to the agenda he and his colleagues had when they suddenly appeared on London's Masonic stage. It stems not only from the document's contents but also from a set of facts *about* it, which is why it is important to our investigation.

The *Old Constitutions* is interesting for several reasons, not the least of which is that it tells us the Masons had a history going back at least to the 1300's. We know this because of the role the document played during the centuries leading up to the Grand Lodge period. Several lodges kept copies of the *Old Constitutions* in their archives, as if they considered it an important and official document. And the Masons accepted Anderson's revised version of it as their official constitution when they finally got around to forming their Grand Lodge. Obviously they thought it told them something they needed to know about their organization.

We might think that this document would also tell us a great deal about the early ritual (which in Masonic terms is often referred to as a "working"), but in fact it doesn't. It contains a history of the craft, a set of "charges," a set of regulations and a few other bits and pieces, but there is little to indicate what the ritual was like.

Then since it doesn't tell us anything about the ritual, how does it fit into our investigation? The importance of the document for us is in a few bits of information which are only implied in its pages. It is our first clue that the newly constituted Masonic lodge, even at this early date, was not really a new organization. It could look back on a long history, and some of its members valued their history very highly indeed.

During the Grand Lodge's first century of existence, the issue of preserving the organization's history caused a great deal of trouble. But it also left behind some of our best clues to the nature of the Fraternity's earliest ritual.

Following those clues will take us north to James Anderson's own country, Scotland, via a rather strange but significant group originally headquartered in London. Strangely, although this organization was founded in London, it has always been called "The Royal Order of *Scotland*," and it holds the key to what Anderson and his allies were trying to accomplish.

Robert Bruce's grave, Dunfermline, Fife, Scotland

On his death in 1329, the reputed protector of the Templars was interred at Dunfermline Abbey. His heart was taken to the Holy Land on Crusade in accordance with his dying wish but was later returned to Scotland and buried at Melrose Abbey.

CHAPTER 2

THE ROYAL ORDER OF SCOTLAND

A Key to the Past

IN the eighteenth century the Royal Order of Scotland was a new Masonic body, but it did not develop as modern readers might expect. Freemasonry is now a stable, well organized fraternity. In the 1700's it was a different animal altogether. And the ritual – the thing that distinguishes one Masonic rite from another – was something else, too.

There are hints in the *Old Constitutions* and other documents from the Grand Lodge's early days that before 1717 the ritual was quite unlike today's version. In fact, while Masonry goes well back into the Middle Ages, the ritual we have now is less than two centuries old. It's a result of what Masons call the Union of 1813. And that brings up another important episode in Masonic history.

The Union of 1813 consisted of a merger of two Grand Lodges commonly referred to as the "Antients" and the "Moderns." The Antients were a group of Masons who followed a governing body known as the "Grand Lodge of England according to the *Old Institutions*." And the "Moderns" were members of what was otherwise called the "Premier Grand Lodge of

England." That's the one we have already discussed, which was formed in 1717.

The Antient Grand Lodge is also known as the "Atholl Grand Lodge," (Atholl being an ancient Earldom in Perthshire, Scotland) and it was formed in part because a number of changes in the ritual and a set of new procedures were being adopted by the Premier Grand Lodge.

A Split in the Ranks

Although the Antients were not formed until July of 1751, the dispute that caused the split had been brewing for a long time. In fact, a committee was set up, possibly as early as 1739, to consider a response to the flap which occurred when the Grand Lodge changed the passwords used by its lodges.

For the uninitiated, this development may require a brief explanation. Masonic passwords, unlike their military counterparts, are not chosen in the morning for use that night. They are traditional words which carry symbolic meaning and remain unchanged, sometimes for centuries. They are integral parts of the ritual, and changing them is not simply a matter of drawing a new word out of a hat. It is a very serious matter, so the Craft's more conservative members must have bristled at what they considered an unwarranted tampering with almost sacred traditions.

The avowed reason for changing the passwords was simple enough. The old ones had been revealed to the public in exposés of the Masonic ritual. Several of these exposés appeared in England at that time, and the Masons were especially concerned about one called *"Masonry Dissected"*. It was published by a man named Samuel Prichard in 1730 and apparently contained all the passwords and recognition signs any Mason needed to gain admission to a lodge meeting.

Once the public knew the passwords, they might masquerade as members and try to infiltrate meetings. Of course, a situation like that is a serious concern for any secret society, so the Grand Lodge decided they had a problem and adopting a new set of passwords was the best way to solve it.

But few things about Masonic history are that simple. Passwords were not the only things changing in the Masonic community. The Craft was in a state of flux, and more than a few of its members were dissatisfied.

That's when the Antient Grand Lodge appeared on the scene. It got off to a modest start, but how it started is something of a mystery. During the twentieth century, the prevailing view among historians has been that it was launched by a group of Irish craftsmen who had come to London looking for work. They found themselves unwelcome in the English Masonic establishment, partly because of their low social standing and partly because they refused to accept the changes in the ritual the English lodges had adopted. They decided to hold onto the version of Masonry they had known in Ireland, so they set up half a dozen lodges and on July 17, 1751 met in the Turk's Head Tavern to organize their own Grand Lodge.

The group was ably led by its first Grand Master, Laurence Dermott, who became a Mason in Dublin in 1741 and served as a lodge master there in 1746. He came to London to work as a painter but soon developed a successful wine business and by all accounts he had a forceful personality and ample administrative ability.

With an inauspicious start but good leadership, the new Grand Lodge prospered from the beginning. Soon, however, what started as a small, provincial effort began finding support from unexpected quarters. It apparently became a magnet for Masons throughout England who were dissatisfied with the changes they saw occurring in their Fraternity. The Antient Grand Lodge eventually grew to 359 lodges, and the glue that held them together was a commitment to the "*Old Constitutions*" with which the Premier Grand Lodge was tampering.

The Antients mocked the followers of the Premier Grand Lodge by calling them "Moderns." It was originally a comment on the innovations the Craft's ruling body was adopting. But in time the members of the older Grand Lodge accepted the term, and that's how they have been known ever since.

These two Masonic bodies rivaled each other from 1751 until 1813, when they finally merged to form a single body. But theirs was not the only dispute going on among the Masons of the British Isles.

While the Schism of 1751 is one of the better known episodes in Masonic history, what is less known is that Freemasonry was badly fragmented during the entire period. No fewer than five Grand Lodges sprang up, each claiming a right to represent the Fraternity.

A Proliferation of Grand Lodges

The Grand Lodge of All England at York was formed in 1725. This body had actually been active in Yorkshire for some time; their records go back to 1705. But they had never been anything other than a small, local operation. That is, they were small and local until they were spurred to greater ambitions.

When the Premier Grand Lodge became successful, the Masons of Yorkshire decided to declare themselves a Grand Lodge, too. They were active for a while but by 1740 they had pretty much ground to a halt and there was little interest for the next twenty years. Then, in 1761, the Premier Grand Lodge issued a warrant for a lodge to meet at the Punch Bowl Tavern in York. That produced enough rivalry to get the York Grand Lodge going again. It quickly set up fourteen lodges in Yorkshire and the surrounding counties and actually functioned as a ruling body for several years.

The lodges in this constituency held on until the 1790's, when they ground to a halt once more, and this time they never became active again. (The official date of their demise is 1792.)

For its part, the York Grand Lodge left some records behind, but its ritual has disappeared. That's a pity from our point of view, because this particular ritual, according to some, was the most ancient and purest version of all, and it certainly would have given us a boost in our search for the original Masonic ritual.

Another organization, the Grand Lodge of England South of the River Trent, was established in 1779. It was the result of a split among the members of a lodge that met at the Goose and Gridiron, and thereby hangs a tale. This lodge was the first of the old lodges who got together to form the Premier Grand Lodge. It was an operative lodge whose origins are unknown, but it was designated No. 1 because it was apparently the oldest of London's Masonic bodies.

When it broke apart, one of its most prominent members, Past Master William Preston, led a group in withdrawing from the Grand Lodge and setting up their own independent body. Preston obtained a charter from the Grand Lodge at York, presumably in deference to that city's reputation as the wellspring of English Masonry, and the Grand Lodge of England South of the River Trent was in business. It continued to operate as a separate Grand Lodge until 1789, when it once again accepted the authority of the Premier Grand Lodge and became just another of its members. Since then this lodge has been called the Lodge of Antiquity, the name it used back in 1760 before its breakup.

It is interesting that this body has a certain distinction among its peers. When the Antients got organized, they gave their lodges numbers, starting with No. 1. Meanwhile, the Moderns continued using their numbering system. So until the Grand Lodges reunited, the Masons of England had two lodges claiming each number.

One provision of the Union of 1813 was that the lodges of the Antients and Moderns would be re-numbered to insure that the oldest received the lowest numbers. On that occasion, the Lodge of Antiquity drew lots for No. 1 and lost. So while its members claimed, and certainly believed, that they deserved to be No. 1, they had to settle for No. 2.

In other words, the Lodge of Antiquity claimed – and everyone took the claim seriously – that it was the oldest lodge around. As evidence of its great age, it still has a copy of the *Old Constitutions* made in 1686. And we must not forget that this lodge was given the honor of hosting the meeting at which the Premier Grand Lodge was formed. That alone shows that the Masonic community had great respect for it.

The relative ages of London's lodges will assume some importance later, but for the moment, we will set that particular dispute aside and return to the other Grand Lodges which arose during this period.

The Scots Grand Lodge in London was formed in 1770. This body was otherwise known as the Supreme Grand Lodge and was a splinter group of the Antients. Its story, as the name implies, has to do with Masons from north of the border.

Lodge No. 50 of the Antient Grand Lodge was composed mostly of Scotsmen. In 1757 it bought the charter of Lodge No. 9, which was officially formed in 1752 but was dropped two years later for non-payment of dues. By acquiring a new charter in this way, Lodge No. 50 earned the right to call itself Lodge No. 9, thus giving itself a lower number, which in Masonic terms is desirable because it implies greater age.

Meanwhile, Lodge No. 54 did essentially the same thing. This lodge was also composed mostly of Scotsmen, and in December of 1756 it bought the charter of Lodge No. 12 for the price of one guinea and thereby lowered its number. (Like the original No. 9, Lodge No. 12 was chartered in 1752 and dropped for non-payment of dues in 1754.)

Now this is where the plot thickens. In 1761 Lodge No. 9 withdrew from the Antients on the pretext that one of its members, a man called Charles Stewart, had lost an election for the office of Junior Grand Warden.

According to the minutes of the Antient Grand Lodge, the incident occurred during its meeting of December 5, 1759. On that occasion, Charles Stewart and one William Dickey were nominated for Junior Warden. Dickey received thirty votes to Stewart's eighteen and thus earned the office for the ensuing year.

So far, the proceedings seem to have been perfectly normal. Grand Lodge officers are routinely elected on an annual basis, and the matter is usually conducted in a cordial and fraternal atmosphere. But for some reason the results of this election produced a bitter argument. Stewart and his supporters disputed the issue vigorously, at one point going so far as threatening to withhold their lodge's financial support from the Grand Lodge.

All of this may have been just a case of sour grapes, but the fact that No. 9's members were mostly Scottish calls our attention to another possibility. Tensions between Scotland and England were still running high, and it is conceivable that those tensions erupted in the lodge room on this one occasion. The vote was scarcely close enough to warrant an appeal, and although Masons do take their lodge politics seriously, it is hard to understand the commotion unless the issue was complicated by something intruding from outside the lodge.

Whatever the cause of the dispute, it didn't end there. A third lodge, No. 59, soon got into the act. Also largely Scottish, it was dropped from the roll of the Grand Lodge three years later.

Surviving records indicate that these three lodges had been closely associated for some time. Members and officers of each lodge visited the others frequently – in fact at almost every meeting. The lodges apparently exchanged dinner invitations, and their relations are consistently portrayed as friendly.

On September 12, 1770 it was proposed that these lodges (Nos. 9, 12, and 59) form their own Grand Lodge. And they did. Three months later they were a new organization and soon grew to five lodges, but they had little success and broke up a few years after that.

In 1775 Lodge No. 12 rejoined the Antients. Three of its sister lodges quickly followed suit, while Lodge No. 59 joined the Moderns.

It is worthwhile to note that during its short life the Supreme Grand Lodge became the first Masonic organization to give its member lodges names as well as numbers. The practice is now standard throughout the Fraternity, but these predominantly Scottish lodges were the first to use proper names. And the names they chose – St. John's, St. David's, St. Andrew's – tended to link them even more closely with Scotland.

The "Why" of the Schism

All of this squabbling and reorganizing would normally be of interest only to Masons and a few historians. It really is an obscure bit of history. But for our purposes it also raises an important question. In spite of the fact that the Masons are an ancient organization, it took them until 1717 to create their first Grand Lodge. So why did a second Grand Lodge appear so soon after the first? And why did a third, fourth and fifth follow so quickly?

If there were no problems with the way the Craft was developing, everyone would have been happy to remain a member of the Premier Grand Lodge. After all, there's no reason to fix something that isn't broken.

The fact that the Fraternity split into so many factions so quickly shows that at least some of England's Masons were dissatisfied with the way the first Grand Lodge was doing business. That dissatisfaction finally reached a breaking point, and a large part of the membership reacted by rejecting the new procedures the Grand Lodge was adopting.

The most striking example of this was the Antients. As their name implies, they were trying to restore what they considered an older and more traditional version of Freemasonry, from which the new Grand Lodge was beginning to depart.

The Antients objected to the "variations in the established forms" they saw cropping up in Masonic ceremonies. But it was more than just changes in procedural matters that the Antients objected to. Lodge procedures never stood by themselves. They were always underpinned by a body of tradition and philosophy. And that's what the Antients were unwilling to abandon.

In the Middle Ages, masonry had been a Christian institution. Now non-Christians were being admitted to full membership. In addition, St. John's Day was being neglected as a proper day for holding Masonic events. And several "esoteric" bits of the ritual were being changed.

Obviously, all of this affected the way the Fraternity was perceived by its members. But even more serious changes were looming on the horizon.

Some time during the 1720's, the notorious "third degree" of the Masonic initiation appeared. The Craft apparently started with a single degree, which most historians believe was a simple initiation ceremony. It contained nothing fancy and very little that was secret. Then at some point in the late Middle Ages a second degree appeared. But it was only after the Grand Lodge had firmly established itself that the Masons put together a third stage of initiation. And that marked a drastic change in the way they performed the ritual.

Freemasonry has always been an organization that values tradition. As such, it has always attracted more than its share of conservative members. And those members could not have enjoyed seeing the most traditional aspects of their fraternity becoming the object of what they must have regarded as an endless round of tampering.

All of this came to a head in the middle of the eighteenth century, when Freemasonry in England finally reached a state that threatened to tear the Fraternity apart. Things had gotten so bad, in fact, that the Antient and Modern Grand Lodges were unable to repair their difficulties for more than sixty years, which carried the dispute well into the next century.

Of course, both groups wanted to do what was right for the Fraternity. One faction was determined to retain the Craft's older, more established procedures, while the other was equally determined to modernize them. So most Masonic historians describe this as a purely internal clash among the members. But it was more complicated than that.

The watershed event was the Schism of 1751 and, as we have seen, it had to do with tradition. Tradition was an important topic for the Masons because of the peculiar situation in which they found themselves. At this particular moment in history, the members of the Craft found themselves embroiled in circumstances which extended well beyond the city of London, the Masons who lived there, and even the eighteenth century.

In particular, they were involved with a larger problem that went to the heart of what was happening in and to the Craft. If the Masons had merely formed a brand new organization, they would have had no traditions to worry about. And if they had been an old organization lumbering along in the usual way, they would have had no transitions to worry about. But in the eighteenth century, Freemasonry was neither of these. It was an old organization that was suddenly undergoing major changes.

As a result, an organization that had some very old traditions was faced with the problem of deciding which traditions to keep and which to modify or abandon altogether. In this kind of situation, the members had no choice but to pay considerable attention to the basics of Freemasonry ... as soon as they figured out precisely what those "basics" were. And that in a nutshell is what the Schism of 1751 was all about.

The Big Picture

Establishing the essential nature of Freemasonry, like everything else in this area, was more complicated than we might imagine. And understanding the process from our modern perspective is equally complicated.

Most of the scholars who studied the topic during the past two and a half centuries were Masons. They were understandably concerned with the internal (i.e. Masonic) aspects of the schism and usually paid little attention to what was going on outside the Fraternity. But during the 1720's, when Masonry was beginning to experience the most significant changes in its history, much of what was happening inside the Craft was influenced by events unfolding across England and Scotland.

What was happening in the country, of course, went far beyond the lodge. So to get a complete picture of the schism, we must go outside the Fraternity and take a look at the society of which it was only a small part.

Perhaps the first thing that impacted the lodge was the Protestant Reformation, which began in 1517, precisely two centuries before the Grand Lodge appeared. It started in a Europe that, like the Masonic lodge, was undergoing serious transformations. The Crusades had forever changed Europe's perception of itself and the outside world. Then the rise of national identity produced countries in a continent that was previously occupied only by feudal territories. To be sure, both of these were lengthy processes. They lasted centuries, but their consequences were to last even longer.

Among other tings, the temporal and spiritual power of the papacy was slipping. Emerging nations were more independent than feudal barons. They saw themselves as part of a much larger world than the one which had previously been ruled by the Church. And the religious hierarchy's perceived greed and corruption led many people to wonder if there was a better way to move forward.

In October 1517, a German monk by the name of Martin Luther brought all of this to a head by leading a revolt. He started by complaining about the sale of papal indulgences, but the issues he raised covered a much broader spectrum. He questioned Church authority across the board and opened the door to secular princes and merchants who were just waiting for an opportunity to expand their own operations.

Luther's ideas took hold quickly in northern Europe. By 1525, the heads of state in several key German principalities had come on board, and they were joined by the king of Denmark and Norway. In short order Luther's teachings formed the spiritual underpinning for a civil war that spread throughout Europe.

The Reformation moved to England in 1532, when Henry VIII split with the Roman Catholic Church over the issue of his divorce from Catherine of Aragon. This was by no means an uncontested divorce. Henry wanted it. The Church didn't. A considerable amount of wrangling ensued, and in the end Henry decided that he had no choice but to leave the Catholic Church and take his whole country with him. In 1534, the English Parliament passed the Act of Supremacy, making the King of England head of the Church in his own country. And that ushered in a wealth of changes.

Of course, Henry did not become a Protestant in the Martin Luther/ John Calvin/John Knox sense of the term. His personal circumstances had more influence on the way his new religion was set up than any fancy foreign preacher could have. Doctrine in the Church of England remained surprisingly similar to what it had been under Catholic rule. The main difference was that the Church of Rome suddenly had less influence in England, and it was that, rather than any theological change, which opened the gate for the Protestant movement to gain momentum there.

Meanwhile in Scotland, the Protestant Reformation was proceeding along more European lines. Following the "martyrdom" of Patrick Hamilton in February 1528, there was increasing pressure for reform. Hamilton was an early reformer, and a very charming one at that. When he was burned at the stake in an ugly flap that had more to do with politics than theology, the people were incensed. And the fact that the execution was botched and that Hamilton was the first native Scot executed for heresy only increased public resentment.

For a time it looked as if the Catholic Church might make the necessary changes and avoid a full scale reformation, but that never materialized. The Scottish alliance with France kept the lid on things for a few decades more; Scotland and France had always been close, and their traditional ties helped protect Catholic interests. However, the arrival of hellfire Reformers like John Knox (who had spent time in Switzerland with John Calvin) blew the lid off altogether, and by 1560 the Scottish Parliament had established Protestantism as the country's official religion.

In a separate but related development, Scotland and England became a united kingdom in 1603 under James VI of Scotland, who was promptly designated James I of Great Britain. Unlike his Catholic mother Mary, Queen of Scots (who in her day had to endure many of Knox's sermons), James professed the Protestant faith.

The result of all this was that by the beginning of the seventeenth century British society was seriously divided along both political and religious lines. This affected everyone to an extent, but it had a particular impact on the early Masonic lodges. They had grown up in a society that was essentially Catholic, and since their main job was building cathedrals, they were even closer to the Church than most people. As a result, their membership was entirely – or almost entirely – Catholic.

Then during the 1600's, with the Reformation gaining strength, the lodges suddenly expanded their membership. But we have to remember that accepting new members was not just a whim. It was what the lodges had to do to survive when cathedral building died out. So before long, the once all Catholic fraternity was admitting men of other religions, including Protestants. In fact the Protestant king, James VI himself, was probably a Mason. (Although the question of his membership is seriously debated, a document known as the Perth manuscript of 1658 asserts that the king was initiated in the Lodge of Scone and Perth No. 3.)

Conflict in the Lodge

Changing its makeup was a significant transition for an organization whose membership was once homogeneous, and whose procedures were tailored to the needs of a single, uniform group. For a start, a proper respect for the new members required toning down some of the religious elements the lodges had brought with them from the Middle Ages. Although little is known of lodge procedures during those early days, we have every reason to believe that many of them were overtly Catholic in tone if not in substance, and as such they would have offended Protestant and Jewish Masons.

One example is the fact that St. John's Day had long been an important date for Masonic events. This was typical of the Middle Ages, when saints' days were used as convenient pegs for recording important events. Everyone knew the saints' days, and they were easy to remember, so they were considered the most suitable times for holding festivals and other notable celebrations.

But over time the general society began to observe saints' days less and less, and events were scheduled without regard for them. In the lodges, St. John's Day began losing its importance, too. And eventually the Masons virtually abandoned it.

In addition, the ritual itself was evolving into a more general working, modifying many Christian references or leaving them out altogether. As a rule, this was a subtle process. Most of the symbols remained the same. They were just given new interpretations.

This was not too difficult, since many religious symbols are shared by several faiths. The symbols are assigned roughly the same meanings by the various religions; only the way they relate to doctrine is different. So if the details that tie them to a particular religion are left out, the symbols can remain and be interpreted in the light of each person's beliefs, usually with no conflict at all.

Still, the lodge's symbols *were* being altered. And along with individual symbols, the way the ritual is performed was altered, too. Various bits of ritual were left out, passwords rearranged, and the catechisms all members are expected to memorize were largely abandoned.

Many of these issues seem trivial to present day Masons, but at the time they obviously stood at the forefront of a very serious dispute. The craft was turning into something different, and it was perfectly normal for the more conservative members to want to keep older, more traditional ways alive.

It is always more comfortable to sit in familiar surroundings and listen to words that have barely changed for generations. So we can easily understand why many of the Masons disagreed with the proposed changes. But that's where another question arises. The high emotions these issues aroused seem too strong, too much of an overreaction. Unless something else was afoot.

The Jacobite Cause

In fact, more important issues were being contested, and they didn't stop at the lodge door, either. The Catholic James VII and II (so called because he was Scotland's seventh King James and England's second) had the distinction of being England's most unpopular monarch. Everything he did seemed to alienate the people and the nobility, who soon decided they preferred James' daughter Mary and her husband William of Orange, both of whom were Protestant. The king ended up waging an unsuccessful campaign to keep the island under his control. In 1690 the matter was settled once and for all when he lost the battle of the Boyne, thirty miles north of Dublin, after which James went into exile in Paris, while the English Parliament invited William and Mary to rule as monarchs of Great Britain in his place.

The Scots Parliament, which was still in existence at the time, was a little miffed that the English had decided the issue without consulting them, but they subsequently adopted William and Mary, too. The new king and queen faced only token resistance, mainly an armed incident in the Scottish Highlands led by Viscount Dundee. But for the most part the transition went smoothly.

The family relationships between these warring monarchs is too complicated to describe here, but the important point for our story is that William and Mary and their successor, Anne, founded a Protestant dynasty known as the Hanoverians, while the Catholic James and his Stewart successors became known as the Jacobites. (This dynasty is also known as the Stuarts. "Stewart" is the old Scottish spelling, while "Stuart" is a French spelling adopted to make things easier for Mary, Queen of Scots, who was raised in France.)

This is where national politics and lodge affairs came together. Such major events as the toppling of a dynasty could hardly be kept completely outside the lodge room. Like the larger society, the Craft had members with a wide range of political affiliations. There's nothing unusual about that, but in this particular case there was a critical difference. Many Freemasons were not only conservative but Jacobite as well. They supported the exiled Stewart dynasty, and that, in a curious way, added a political dimension to the arguments being waged within the Fraternity.

While James VII lived, he was merely an exiled king. He didn't have enough power or support to stage a comeback. But when he died in 1701, apparently dogged by a depressive illness which had made him such an ineffectual king, the stage was set for a bitter and prolonged conflict. His son and grandson mounted a number of attempts to regain the throne he had effectively thrown away, making the fifty years after the battle of the Boyne a very interesting time in British politics.

The course of those fifty years did not run smoothly. In 1705, the first Jacobite Rebellion fizzled out almost before it began. James VII's son, James Francis Edward (also known as The Old Pretender), turned out to be a pretty uninspiring leader. However, the Jacobite cause rumbled on, partly because it was much larger than one man. In fact, it was more complex than a split between the Scots and the English, or even between Catholics and Protestants. The dispute even had international overtones, since France was always keen to lend a hand in destabilizing the British Government.

With all this at stake, the Jacobites didn't give up. Two years before the Grand Lodge was formed, they staged a second unsuccessful rebellion, but after an inconclusive battle at Sheriffmuir in the Scottish Lowlands, that too fizzled out. Then, thirty years later (in 1745) Charles Edward Stewart, otherwise known as Bonnie Prince Charlie (The Young Pretender), launched one final effort. He sailed from France to Scotland with a few faithful supporters. There, he raised an army of about two thousand men from among the Scottish clans and prepared for battle.

He scored a few victories and marched into England, but the young Stewart prince seems to have lacked the forceful leadership needed to overcome the superior power that lay on the Hanoverian side. He was certainly a charismatic figure. People were eager to follow him, and years later they still remembered him fondly. But at the time he was given poor advice and apparently didn't have the decisive personality required to take charge of his situation.

He was also left high and dry by some of his own supporters. The French Government failed to back up their promises with more than a few men and a couple of ships. And when the Jacobite army marched into England, most pro-Jacobite Englishmen found that they had pressing business elsewhere. All that was left to Prince Charlie was the support of the Highland clans and a few Scottish Lowlanders.

Not to put too fine a point on it, this was pretty much the end of the Jacobites' political aspirations. But conflicts of such magnitude have a way of making themselves felt in other quarters.

Lodge Politics

To an extent, the dispute in the lodge mirrored the political situation in England. Both had to do with the proper role of tradition. Bonnie Prince Charlie appealed to traditionalists who believed that the Stewart dynasty, with its outdated concepts of the divine rights of kings, was still worthy of support.

The Hanoverians, on the other hand, were a more progressive group. They knew the crown had to adapt to the cultural shift which had occurred since the Reformation. With a large measure of political smarts, they moved the country toward a constitutional monarchy, and in doing so found a way of clinging to the trappings of tradition while accommodating change.

This was the climate in which the world's first Grand Lodge was organized. It was also the climate in which the splintering of the Premier Grand Lodge occurred.

Far from being an isolated event, then, the schism in the Masonic community reflected the religious and political divisions in the general society. It primarily expressed itself in the two main competing Grand Lodges. One was conservative, holding to traditional forms that were tied to the days when the Fraternity was still entirely Christian and Catholic. The other was liberal, moving with the times and showing a marked willingness to modify parts of the ritual that didn't fit current circumstances.

Given the intellectual ferment of the eighteenth century, the liberal view was bound to win out. But the more conservative elements took a long time to disappear. The conflict was tied to too many political, religious and philosophical strands from outside the lodge to die easily.

Rancor continued to divide the Fraternity for more than sixty years. But most of the members understood that Freemasonry had always been a single fraternity. It may have been decentralized, and the local lodges may have exercised a great deal of independence, but it was still one organization, held together by a strong spirit of unity that had existed long before anyone could remember.

There was enough of this sense of brotherhood to bring the Craft back together. So while the membership engaged in a series of arguments about the proper way to conduct Masonic affairs, they were also moving toward an agreement that would allow them once again to be a single organization.

In 1809 the Moderns formed the Lodge of Promulgation. That's a fancy name for what amounted to a committee assigned to negotiate a reunion with the Antients. This lodge stayed in business until 1811, during which time most of its activities consisted of assembling the masters of London's lodges, along with other Masonic dignitaries, and performing the various rituals to determine how they might best be reconciled.

The committee settled on a composite ritual, which consisted mostly of workings performed by the Antients. That was a victory of sorts for the traditionalists, but it wasn't a complete victory. It left one major problem unresolved. In 1813, representatives of the two grand lodges brought the schism to an end by signing the Articles of Union. This document amounted to some twenty-one items, and one of them specified that Masonry would henceforth consist of three degrees.

Simply put, by the time the Grand Lodges finally reunited in the Union of 1813, the Fraternity had gone too far to return to what it had been. Many of the changes the Craft had undergone could not be reversed, and come what may, those changes – including the addition of a third degree – had to be legitimized by being adopted as established forms.

The union, after all, was a compromise. It involved a deliberate shift away from overtly Christian elements, partly to accommodate non-Christian members but also to avoid offending both Catholic and Protestant members with strong feelings about political issues that were still very much a part of current affairs.

So the conservative and Jacobite members saw their fraternity moving away from traditions they held dear. And while many of them accepted the compromises that created the United Grand Lodge of England, they were not completely happy about the way things were going.

Compromises always fall short of satisfying those at the extremes of an argument. Therefore they always stop short of completely resolving the problems. And in this case, the compromise set the stage for yet another round of fiddling with the ritual.

The Scottish Agenda

This is where that little known rite called the Royal Order of Scotland comes in. The Royal Order has always been considered a minor blip in the history of Masonic degrees, but the role it played in the eighteenth century was much more central than most scholars realize. Indeed, that role may be essential to understanding what the schism was really about.

The origin of the rite is admittedly obscure. If the people who organized it kept any records, they have long since disappeared, and historians are left with only scraps of evidence to piece together how it got started.

The Royal Order of Scotland apparently arose during the second quarter of the eighteenth century, and its degrees may have been written by Andrew Michael Ramsay, an exiled Jacobite who at the time was active in French Masonic affairs.

Ramsay was born in 1686, perhaps in the Scottish town of Ayr. He was well educated, attending Edinburgh University and becoming a member of the prestigious Royal Society. And for a short time he was Bonnie Prince Charlie's tutor.

Ramsay moved to France in 1709 and became a Roman Catholic about a year later. In 1730, he was initiated in Horn Lodge, and this is our first indication that Andrew Michael Ramsay was part of an agenda. Horn Lodge was one of the four old lodges whose members established the Premier Grand Lodge of England. And another member of this particular lodge was the James Anderson who wrote the Grand Lodge's constitution.

Now, admittedly, the fact that two people are members of the same lodge proves nothing. But the timing of this situation is, to say the least, suspicious.

Although the records are sketchy, there is no indication that James Anderson was in any way involved with the formation of the Grand Lodge. In fact, he apparently had nothing to do with it until 1721, when he wrote its *Constitutions*. At that point he was active for a few years, becoming Grand Warden on January 17, 1723 and serving as master of one of the local lodges. Curiously, he seems to have been a member of a number of lodges in London during those years. Then he dropped out of sight (Masonically, at least) until about 1730. That was the same time Ramsay joined one of the lodges where Anderson had been a member and, as we will soon see, it was about the time the ritual of the Royal Order was written, possibly by Ramsay himself.

It seems that these two Scottish Masons were making a habit of showing up at precisely the right times to influence the affairs of the Masonic establishment in London. Indeed, it appears that Anderson may have started something in 1721 and had to call Ramsay in a few years later to help him finish it. Both men were certainly on the scene when the Royal Order of Scotland was organized. And the Order's ritual is thoroughly Scottish, going so far as to set aside an empty chair for Robert Bruce, that country's fourteenth century king and hero. But we're getting ahead of our story.

36

The Royal Order of Scotland seems to have struggled for about a century, until it finally acquired critical mass some time around the 1830's, then it settled down to take a place among Freemasonry's other "advanced" degrees.

However, much of the Order's early history unfolded in London. That may seem a strange place for an overtly Scottish rite to develop, but there is some reason to believe that those early years in London are the key to its very existence.

There had been a Scottish influence in London's lodges for a long time. When Scotland's King James VI was crowned as James I of England in 1603, he moved his royal court from Edinburgh to London. A large number of Scottish politicians and hangers-on came with him, and many of them were Freemasons. (To paraphrase J. M. Barrie, there were few more impressive sights than a Scottish Freemason on the make in London.)

The Scottish newcomers began attending local meetings, thus giving a transfusion of Scottish Masonry to the old London lodges. And although little evidence survives, we can only assume that there was quite an exchange of ideas about Masonic traditions and procedures, with a large dose of northern ideas eventually being accepted by the southern Masons.

In addition, James VI and I (as he was known after his English coronation) was a Stewart. So he and his dynasty were at the heart of the Jacobite cause which was to erupt at the end of the century. In fact, the very term "Jacobite" comes from the Latin word for "James."

And there were other Scottish influences as well. When the Antients arose to challenge the Premier Grand Lodge, many of the issues had to do with ritual matters. The Antients used a ritual that was virtually identical to the ones used in Scotland and Ireland. And their main complaint seemed to be that the "Moderns" were drifting away from that version of the ritual.

We should also remember that the Antients were called "Atholl" Masons. They acquired this name because their Grand Masters during most of the period from 1771 until 1813 were the Dukes of Atholl. Again, this is hardly proof of a conspiracy, but it is one more Scottish connection.

The York Grand Lodge provides yet another Scottish influence, though it is more subtle and elusive. While the York Grand Lodge might have appeared to be purely English, it was connected with a piece of Masonic doggerel called the York Legend. We will soon see how the York Legend is intimately tied up with the origin of Freemasonry, which in turn has a hidden connection with a bit of Scottish history.

And there's one more Scottish connection. We must not forget the tiny Scots Grand Lodge. While the details of their dispute with the rest of the Craft are not clear, it is clear that they were trying to establish a Grand Lodge which was more closely associated with Scotland.

Obviously the Masons of London were engaged in a serious dispute about the basic nature of Freemasonry, and Scotland keeps cropping up in the dispute. It is hardly a coincidence, then, that the Royal Order of Scotland began life during the years leading up to the Schism of 1751, or that it was organized shortly after the third degree appeared on the scene. It is no less a coincidence that the Order's members didn't give up on it during its lean years. In fact, they stuck with their rite through the years following the Union of 1813 and kept working until they made it a viable and permanent organization.

Actually, the success of the Royal Order is more remarkable than it seems. A large number of Masonic rites and degrees appeared during the eighteenth century. They were successful for a while, but the vast majority of them have long since disappeared. Thus the Royal Order's success, not to mention the tenacity of its supporters, is quite impressive. It's so impressive that we might well wonder if there was a special reason why this rite succeeded while most of its contemporaries failed.

When we look a little deeper, we find that there's a very good reason to believe this rite was special. It was organized by a small group of dissident Masons who were reacting to the legend of the third degree and who were apparently bent on preserving a legend they considered the true story of the first Masons.

The First Masons?

The Royal Order's ritual actually tells us as much. It says that the rite was established on Mt. Moriah and later re-established at Kilwinning in order to "correct the errors and reform the abuses which had crept in among the three Degrees of St. John's Masonry."

On the surface, that may sound reasonable enough. But when we take a closer look, we encounter a curious problem.

The Royal Order's ritual says that the king of Scotland first sat as Grand Master at Kilwinning. But if that's true, it had to happen at an early date. The king in question was supposedly Robert Bruce, whose reign lasted from 1306 until 1329. So we would have to assume that the Royal Order was re-established during those years.

However, it is well known that Masonic degrees take liberties with their legends. If we allow for a little poetic license and assume that the ritual actually refers to some other Scottish king, we could be talking about a much later date. But we are still limited to a time before 1625, which marked the end of the reign of James VI and I. He was the last king of Scotland.

What are we to make of that? After 1625, the Order could not have had a Scottish king as its Grand Master. But if the Order was re-established at any time before 1625, there simply could not have been three Masonic degrees. The third degree did not come into existence until the 1720's.

Obviously we have encountered an enigma. And if this is more than a careless mistake by the Masons who wrote the ritual, it may be important.

It seems that if we are to understand the Royal Order properly, we must look for something that happened to an existing organization, as indicated by the term "re-established." But it happened after the third degree was created, and it was done specifically to return the ritual to the form it took prior to the changes and compromises that occurred during the 1700's.

This is underscored by the reference to Kilwinning, which obviously associates the Order with the antiquity of the old, medieval craft. This reference is not surprising by itself. It was customary at that time for social organizations to claim ancient pedigrees as a way of giving themselves a little extra prestige.

The lineage described in the *Old Constitutions* is an example of this. It claims that the Fraternity descended from such notable and ancient gentlemen as Adam (who is described as creating the craft of architecture), Noah, Moses and the like. When James Anderson decided to include this list in his *Constitutions*, he was simply reaching back to the oldest pedigree possible, without an excessive concern for historical accuracy.

To an extent, the Masons who wrote the ritual for the Royal Order of Scotland were merely following accepted practice in this regard. But that same ritual contains details which suggest something else was afoot.

The reference to the kings of Scotland appears to be an attempt to preserve a bit of genuine history, particularly since the Order originated in London. If English Masons were creating a legend that had nothing to do with real history, they would have said less about their old enemy Scotland and made more of the Order's supposed association with Mt. Moriah, the famous temple mount at Jerusalem. That little piece of real estate has always been associated with King Solomon's Temple, which is the main setting for the third degree and is a perfectly natural spot for Masons to celebrate in their rituals.

Claiming a connection with Kilwinning may, of course, be nothing more than a way of asserting great age, and it may have nothing to do with anything else. The lodge at Kilwinning was undoubtedly the oldest in Scotland, probably the oldest in the world, and everyone knew it. However, if the Royal Order's ritual is in some way tied to actual history, we must view these references to Scotland and Scotland's king as clues to the Order's beginnings. And this takes us back to the rituals that were used before the eighteenth century.

Kilwinnig Abbey

Built by French stone masons during the 12th century, this abbey's construction site was reputedly the location of the world's first masonic lodge. The building was destroyed during the Protestant Reformation.

Shades of the Medieval Ritual

One thing we know about the rituals of the pre-Grand Lodge era is that they show a great deal of variety. For a start, the early Masons used more than one password. Some were variations of the same word, but others were completely different. And there were a number of recognition signs, not all of which would have been used at the same time.

Scholars agree that these variations prove one thing. Although there was a single ritual, by the 1600's it had evolved into several versions. And that tells us something about the organization.

The fact that there are so many variations in the early ritual is our best evidence of what Masonry was like in its early days. It tells us that the craft no longer had a standard, universally accepted ritual during the years before the first Grand Lodge was established. And since many of the oldest workings were certainly lost or destroyed over the years, we can conclude that there were even more variations than we know about. So Freemasonry must have been a very diverse organization as it emerged from the Middle Ages.

This is precisely what we would expect from a mostly illiterate society in which travel and communications were painfully slow. And in the mountains of Scotland, where isolation was often as much a matter of pride as a practical concern, we can easily imagine that lodges operated and evolved with a minimum of influence from their neighbors.

The logical result of such a process was, quite naturally, a fragmented fraternity, which isn't surprising, because we can see something similar in today's world. Even now, several lodges and rites are considered, in Masonic jargon, "irregular." Although they claim to be fully Masonic, their pedigrees, which often lack Grand Lodge affiliation, keep them from being recognized by other bodies.

In medieval Scotland, where clannishness was another point of pride, we must assume that the craft was even more decentralized. This is not to say that splinter groups had drifted away from the established forms. It is rather to say that what the Masons of the day meant by "established forms" might have been a real issue.

The issue was one of the matters settled when the Grand Lodge was established. As a ruling body, it got the individual lodges organized and worked out uniform procedures for everyone to follow.

But innovations often take hold only when all the supporters of the old ways have died. And in the mid-1700's, when supporters of the older workings were still around, there must have been a large number of Masons who were simply unwilling to abandon the version of Masonry they had known all their lives. In addition, the Jacobite conspiracies and rebellions must have played a role in the disputes that arose among lodge members throughout the kingdom. Although the Craft has traditionally banned political discussions inside the lodge, people can not leave their feelings and loyalties outside when they enter a room.

Thus, when the Fraternity moved toward a standard ritual and tried to reconcile its many traditions and variations, the inevitable result was a round of serious conflict. As the old craft evolved into a modern social club – and one with a more general membership as well – many of the old forms were endangered. They no longer fitted what the organization had become. Or if they did fit, so many members objected to them that they had to be modified. Then, after decades of arguing, the whole affair was resolved by a compromise that called for abandoning even more of the old workings.

At that point, the champions of the old ways were scarcely inclined to forsake their long held traditions and practices in favor of "new fangled" elements in the ritual. In short, when the Union of 1813 took even more steps to modernize and transform the Fraternity, the Craft still had an ardent faction who were determined to prevent the older, more traditional landmarks from ceasing to exist.

By its own admission, the legacy of that faction was the Royal Order of Scotland. Its ritual describes itself as an effort to return to the older workings. But in Freemasonry, where history is unashamedly and seamlessly blended with legend, is there any evidence that the Royal Order's ritual contains anything more than a legend created out of whole cloth in the late eighteenth century?

There are several clues that it does, and the most obvious are the ones that lie on the surface. First, the Royal Order is a Christian rite. By all accounts the original Masonic lodge was Christian in form if not exclusively in membership.

43

Second, the Royal Order has two degrees. Though the medieval lodge seems to have started with a single degree, by the end of the seventeenth century it had devised a second degree. That was the way the ritual was when it emerged from the Middle Ages. And after the third degree was added, a system of two degrees is what conservative Masons would have looked back on and considered the legitimate form of the ritual.

But this doesn't prove anything about the Royal Order's history. Masons in the eighteenth century must have known about the Craft's Christian origins and two-degree system. These were well established bits of history. So just as the other "advanced" degrees added Old Testament and Templar stories to their rituals, the Royal Order might simply have included bits of Masonic history in its ritual.

Legend or History

What lends an air of authenticity to Royal Order's claims is the subtle way they relate to issues current in the Fraternity during the days leading up to the schism. To begin with, the Grand Lodge of England was founded on the 24th of June (St. John's Day) in 1717. On the face of it, that could be an arbitrary date. St. John's Day was, after all, the traditional time for important Masonic events.

But we must remember that the observance of St. John's Day was one of the issues that led to the schism. It was originally *the* day for Masonic assemblies. Then, as the eighteenth century wore on, fewer and fewer events were held on this day, and the more conservative Masons objected strongly.

Since the dispute was about tradition, we must wonder what tradition made St. John's Day so important. Here, the Royal Order of *Scotland* provides the answer. It made a point of honoring Robert Bruce by saving a seat for him four centuries after his death. The most important event of

Bruce's life was the battle of Bannockburn. And that battle took place on St. John's Day in 1314.

It is interesting that the founders of the Grand Lodge missed the 400th anniversary of Bannockburn by only three years. Of course, there is no evidence that the battle had any special meaning to the four old lodges in London. But anyone who is familiar with the difficulties of starting a new organization, and who understands the slow pace of life in the eighteenth century, can agree that a delay of three years is insignificant. In addition, the Jacobite Rebellion of 1715 had put the whole country in a state of turmoil. One of its after effects was the execution of the revolution's leaders, which was not finished until early 1717. This bit of commotion in itself would have been a good reason for any "secret" society to keep a low profile. So it is quite possible that the Masons really did pick the 400th anniversary of Bannockburn as the day on which they wanted to found their Grand Lodge but were delayed by unavoidable circumstances.

Nevertheless, why would English Masons want to commemorate a Scottish victory over their own ancestors? In the early eighteenth century, the subject of Scottish independence could still rouse strong emotions on both sides of the border.

Scotland and England may have had the same king after 1603, but they had separate Parliaments until 1707. That was when the Act of Union merged the Scottish and English Parliaments into a single body. But the move was vigorously opposed north of the border. Like all political doings, it included an element of "pump priming" on the part of some Scottish leaders, which by itself inspired popular resentment.

In addition, many Scots felt the move had been forced on them, and they didn't like the consequences. The English erected trade barriers until the Scottish economy began to disintegrate. Old antagonism against a more powerful neighbor continued to simmer, despite the politicians' assurances that all was well. And the political climate became so sensitive that outbreaks of hostility could stem from even minor incidents.

As late as 1736, one incident in Edinburgh known as the Porteous Riot nearly caused Queen Anne to revoke the ancient capital's privileges as a Royal Burgh. Following the hanging of a thief who was popular with the locals, the Captain of Edinburgh's Town Guard, one John Porteous, fired on an unruly mob. He was convicted of murder in the Scottish Court but was quickly granted a stay of execution by the Hanoverian queen in London. An Edinburgh mob then took the law into its own hands and rioted, dragging the hapless Porteous from the city jail and hanging him on a dyer's pole.

Of course, this incident had to do with more than a lovable rogue and police brutality. The real issue was one of sovereignty. Queen Anne took badly to having her wishes overruled by a Scottish rabble, while the Scottish rabble felt much the same about the specter of a distant, half-German monarch meddling in what they saw as their affairs. If the queen had pulled Edinburgh's royal charter, even more violence would have followed.

Although the Jacobite cause was to run out of steam after 1745, clashes between Jacobites and Hanoverians were by no means on the decline during the early years of the century. They continued to cut across political lines throughout the country, with old disputes still having the power to rouse strong feelings.

The Masons of London would have known all about these issues. And in such a tense setting, they would have needed a good reason for pinning the establishment of any organization of theirs to a date connected with Scottish independence.

The Royal Order's tribute to Robert Bruce is a clue that they may have had an excellent reason. By paying homage to Bruce, they connected their rite to a theory that became popular in the mid-eighteenth century – the theory that Freemasonry descended from the chivalric Orders of knighthood which had arisen during the Crusades.

Melrose Abbey, Scottish Borders

Robert Bruce's heart was buried in this abbey following an aborted attempt to carry it to the Holy Land in fulfilment of his dying wish.

That theory, in turn, dovetails with a persistent theory from outside Masonry. And the two, taken together, reveal what the founders of the Royal Order were trying to accomplish.

The more general theory deals with the Knights Templar, whose Order was supposedly disbanded only a few years before the battle of Bannockburn. According to this theory, some of the Templars refused to let their organization die. Instead, they split up and went underground. One group fled to Scotland, where they joined forces with Robert Bruce and turned the tide of battle by charging onto the field at the head of a reserve division.

This idea is quite controversial, but it is supported by enticing snippets of history. Contemporary accounts say that reserves did charge onto the field at Bannockburn, waving a sheet and thus causing panic among the English troops. Some historians argue that the sheet – ordinarily a curious thing to wave on such an occasion – was actually the Templars' black and white banner, or possibly the all-white banner the Arab armies used when they charged into battle.

And there is the strange case of Alexander Seton, who went over to the Scottish side the night before the battle and brought vital information about the English army with him. Some historians claim Seton was a Templar spy, citing the fact that he was later described as "Frater Alexander de Seton miles, hospitalis Sancti Johannis Jerusalem in Scotia," namely a Friar of the Knights Hospitaller, the Order which inherited Templar lands in Scotland after the Templars were officially disbanded.

Then there is perhaps a more telling incident: when King Robert Bruce lay dying in 1329, he asked his closest friends to help him fulfill a vow he had made "when he had most ado" to defend his realm. He told them to remove his heart when he died, take it with them to the Holy Land and carry into battle against the Saracens.

It is hard to understand why Bruce would have been preoccupied with thoughts of the Crusades during what he called the most hectic period of his career. Or perhaps we should say it's hard to understand unless the vow he made on that occasion was part of an alliance with the Templars, who themselves must have longed to fight again in the Holy Land.

These are isolated facts which by themselves prove little. But they do serve as the starting point for building a case that Robert Bruce and the Templars had dealings that never quite made it into the history books.

The non-Masonic theory ends there, while the Royal Order takes the matter a step further. It claims that it was established after Bannockburn, when Bruce himself created a new Order of knighthood to reward a group of Masons who had helped him win the battle.

But at this point the theory becomes a riddle. How could operative masons, presumably the only kind in existence at the time, have provided such exemplary service in the battle?

There were no stone fortifications at Bannockburn, and nothing else the masons could have built for the occasion. Besides, the position stone masons occupied in medieval society – exalted as they were above the peasants – still makes it doubtful that anyone would consider them suited for knighthood.

We will have more to say about the curious issue of knighthood in the next chapter, but for the moment we need to decide who these "masons" were. If it wasn't operative stone masons who helped save the day at Bannockburn, this legend must be a veiled account of some other group who performed an uncommon feat. And the only other group for which that claim has been made is the fugitive Templars. Was that what the Freemasons of London were commemorating when they chose the 24th of June as the date for opening their Grand Lodge?

Indeed, some of the Masons active in London and elsewhere during that period were Scots. They included James Anderson, who composed their book of constitutions, and Andrew Ramsay, who later served as Orator of the Grand Lodge of France. These Scots seem to have been the ones pushing a connection with the Crusades. And Ramsay, in particular, is credited with introducing the idea that the Masons descended from the Crusader knights.

This occurred during the oration for which Ramsay is best known today. He first delivered his oration at a Lodge in Paris during December of 1736, then he presented a revised version of it to the Grand Lodge of France on March 21 of the following year.

Ramsay's contribution of the Templar legend to Masonic lore is generally considered an innovation, but it may have been quite the opposite. It may have been an attempt to preserve something that was in danger of being lost.

It is difficult to see what Ramsay was up to simply by looking at his speech. But if we consider the dispute that was going on just across the English Channel, we can see that Ramsay may have been touting an obscure bit of Scottish history. Apparently he thought Freemasonry was the proper custodian for it. However, the sudden appearance of this subject on the Masonic scene requires more explanation than that.

Fortunately, a good explanation is not hard to find. The self proclaimed history of the Royal Order of Scotland shows precisely what Ramsay's motives were.

The Royal Order claims in its ritual that the king of Scotland first sat as its Grand Master at Kilwinning. As we have said, this statement was partly intended to give the organization a pedigree dating back to the Middle Ages, but it serves another purpose as well. The same passage tells us that the Order did not originate with the kings of Scotland. It began on Mt. Moriah before it ever met at Kilwinning.

These are carefully chosen words that tell a story: the king of Scotland became the leader of an organization which existed long before he was involved with it. This king was Robert Bruce, and the Order was first established on Mt. Moriah (the temple mount in Jerusalem) before moving to Scotland.

Since the Templars did in fact establish their first headquarters on Jerusalem's temple mount, this story implies very strongly that the Royal Order of Scotland began life as the band of fugitive Templars who allegedly supported Bruce that day at Bannockburn.

This finally reveals the real issue swirling at the center of the Masonic dispute. In the eighteenth century, Robert Bruce was not just a figure from ancient history. His daughter Marjorie had married Walter the Steward, a union that marked the beginning of the Stewart dynasty, which the Jacobites were still defending so passionately in the early 1700's.

If Bruce really did found a new Order of chivalry to reward Templars who helped him win the battle, and if Freemasonry – at least in Scotland – descended from that Order, the Scottish lodges would certainly have preserved the story of the event in their ritual. And if the Scottish Masons did have a Templar legend dating back to the days of Robert Bruce, they would certainly have wanted to keep it alive.

A legend tied to both the pivotal event of Scottish independence and the beginnings of Freemasonry? Something like that would lie at the very heart of a heritage the patriotic Scots of the day were struggling to preserve. And tampering with a legend of such magnitude would have been more than enough to precipitate a schism among the Masons of eighteenth century London.

Any Templar legend which did exist at the time was left out of the three degree system that developed during the Grand Lodge's early years. The liberal wing of the Craft must have decided that claiming Templar origins was too "Catholic," or at least too "Christian," for the general membership their fraternity had acquired. But they may have tried to reach out to the legend's supporters.

It was just about this time that the Hiramic section of the ritual appeared. It tells the legendary story of the Craft's origins and is often interpreted as a veiled account of the Templars' later history. But if this story is about the Templars, it is so couched in symbolism that it is unrecognizable.

Perhaps retelling the Templar legend in symbolic form was a concession to the more traditional members of the lodge, but it didn't go far enough. Those conservative Scots considered their heritage too important to be altered in such a way, because to them it lay at the heart of both an ancient rite and a prized bit of history.

And they had a point. If a Templar legend was part of an older, medieval set of workings, we can be sure from its great age that it was close to the original spirit of Masonry. It was not a mere extra but was, at least in the eyes of the more traditional Masons of the eighteenth century, an essential part of the Craft's heritage.

The details of the Royal Order's ritual, taken together with the history of the dispute that led up to the Schism of 1751, strongly suggest that there really was a bit of history in the Masonic ritual as it emerged from the Middle Ages. And if this is true, the Craft's connection with the Crusader knights was not something Ramsay invented. It was an important part of Freemasonry's heritage and was in danger of being lost.

The Scottish Masons who frequented London and Paris during the eighteenth century considered themselves the custodians of the true Masonic "secret." It was the story of a band of fugitive knights who made common cause with the future king of Scotland and, by taking the field at Bannockburn, changed Scottish history and gave birth to a new secret Order. It was secret at first for practical reasons. But as time went on, its secrecy was preserved as a matter of long held tradition.

And since the victory at Bannockburn also paved the way for the creation of the Stewart dynasty, it was not just a matter of fraternal interest. It was a serious part of British politics as well.

Even centuries later, those conservative Scots were unwilling to reveal their secret fully. They still told a veiled version of the story, claiming it was "masons" who came to the Bruce's aid. But they knew the truth behind the fiction, and they were not willing to compromise the story when their ancient Order evolved into a modern fraternity. For them it was something they had to save.

Seen in this light, the Schism of 1751 was not merely a dispute over such minor issues as meeting dates and admitting new members. It was a struggle to preserve a legend some considered the essence of their Masonic heritage. And the Union of 1813 was not merely a compromise to bring two factions together again. It was a watershed that changed the Fraternity forever. It left the supporters of the old craft so dissatisfied they had to create another rite to keep their legend alive.

By this time, the Jacobite cause may have been a spent force in British politics, but it was still important to Scottish Masons of the old school.

The evidence shows that the Royal Order's degrees were written by one of those Scottish Masons around 1730. This was shortly after the third degree and the Hiramic legend appeared. It was a time when the Masonic ritual was being refashioned. And the results of those changes – especially in such a conservative organization as the Masons – could be expected to define Masonic lore for as long as anyone could predict.

The Royal Order's degrees were an attempt to take the ritual back to what its writer believed was a more legitimate form. The degrees insisted that it was Scotland, not Jerusalem, to which the Masons owed the origin of their craft. And they named the man who gave the Fraternity a new start.

There is every reason to believe that the Royal Order's degrees were heir to an older, medieval ritual which claimed that Masonry really did emerge from the bloody field of Bannockburn. This is no less a claim than that the same blood which gave birth to three hundred years of Scottish independence and the Stewart kings also brought the world's foremost fraternity into existence.

When it at last became clear that this claim would no longer be part of the evolving fraternity's heritage, its champions were determined to preserve it the only way they could. During the generation following the Union of 1813, they struggled to keep their legend alive in the initiation ritual of the Royal Order of Scotland. And in the rite's survival, they preserved a story which had been told in the glens of Scotland for centuries but was rejected, like an oddly shaped building stone that didn't quite fit, by a craft whose members were now looking to the future.

CHAPTER 3

A MYSTERIOUS FORCE

Bannockburn, 1314.

THE importance of the legend preserved by the Royal Order of Scotland is that it brings us several centuries closer to the origins of the Masonic ritual. Everyone agrees that the Masons had a ritual before the Grand Lodge was established in 1717, but only traces of it have survived. They give us little historic information and, unfortunately, the Craft's "official" history tells us nothing about how it all began.

It is only the Royal Order, with its self avowed mission of preserving the pure form of the ritual, that tells us how Freemasonry arose in the British Isles. And their version of the story directs our attention to an ancient Scottish battle, the details of which will bring us a step closer to the end of our quest.

The battle of Bannockburn, like all battles, was not a pretty piece of pageantry for the men involved. The two armies clashed in desperate hand-to-hand combat just after dawn, then they continued fighting through the morning and afternoon of a hot, sweltering midsummer's day.

The Scottish king, Robert Bruce, used what historians consider a new found tactical genius. His earlier campaigns were lackluster, and it was only in the previous few years that Bruce had changed his strategy and started scoring impressive victories.

On this occasion, he chose to start the battle in a defensive position, perched on top of a piece of naturally rising ground. His small force of lightly armed, nimble horsemen under Robert Keith took care of the English archers. Then a sudden advance by Bruce's foot soldiers made the opposition's heavy cavalry an encumbrance instead of the deadly weapon it usually was.

The revolutionary nature of this last tactic is hard to appreciate now. In a mediaeval army of this period, the infantry was expected to stand still while enemy horses had a jolly good gallop at it, usually with fatal results for the foot soldiers. If that failed, a devastating hail of arrows from the archers could be expected to break the infantry's ranks in advance of another cavalry charge.

Bruce's two masterstrokes rewrote the rulebook. But he still had a lot to worry about. For one thing, he was seriously outnumbered.

Estimates vary as to the size of the armies that day, although the proportions are generally consistent. Barbour, the earliest Scottish chronicler, puts the English army at 100,000 men, with the Scots at 30,000. (Curiously, he adds that the Scots had another twenty thousand "small folk" and camp followers whom Bruce sent away from the battlefield before the fighting commenced, a detail whose importance will soon become obvious.)

More modern estimates put the numbers at 20,000 English to 8,000 Scots. But whichever figure we believe, the odds are about the same: three to one against Scotland.

The dawn advance evened the odds a little. The English had camped in a loop of the river, and the Scots managed to pin them in that tight space. Behind the English and to their sides, a deep gorge made either a tactical withdrawal or a flanking maneuver impossible. In front, the Scots threw four divisions into the battle, one by one. The only way forward was through them. So instead of a jolly good gallop, the English knights found themselves fighting with Scottish pikemen, while their wounded and frightened horses caused havoc in their own ranks.

But the sheer weight of numbers was now making it impossible for the smaller army to press home its advantage. The English might still have recovered. If they had been able to break the ranks of the tiring enemy at any point, their superior numbers would have won the day. But just at that point, a strange incident turned the battle in favor of the Scots once and for all. As if from nowhere, a mysterious force suddenly appeared.

According to Barbour, around 15,000 of the "yeomen, swains, and camp-followers" who had been left minding the cooking pots suddenly elected a captain from among their number, made banners out of "broad sheets" and charged onto the field of battle. The English, seeing this fresh force of Scottish rabble, began to waver, whereupon the Scots' regular troops pressed them all the harder. Within a short space of time, the English nerve failed altogether and the Scottish advance turned into a rout.

The English commander, King Edward II, escaped capture by the skin of his teeth. And a battle he should have won turned out to be one of his worst defeats.

But Barbour's account of these extra troops has an odd feel to it. His version of the battle has never been seriously questioned. It is a remarkably objective account, and even modern historians have nothing but praise for it. Still, the romantic idea of 15,000 cooks and bottle washers suddenly appearing to win the day for a seriously outnumbered Scottish army? There are a couple of problems with that notion.

The first problem is that it simply isn't credible for Bruce, heavily outnumbered as he was, to leave such a large force of able-bodied men minding the cooking pots. Even ignoring Barbour's apparently inflated numbers, it's obvious that his "small folk" would have increased the Scottish army by about fifty percent.

True, armies have always required large numbers of support personnel, and ancient and medieval armies in particular were accompanied by quite a few camp followers. But they tended to be women or men who were too young, old or infirm to fight.

In highly organized units, such as the ancient Roman legions or even Edward II's forces, the people in the baggage train would certainly have been kept behind the lines. But we must not forget that Bruce didn't have that kind of army. He stood at the head of a loosely organized band of what some would describe as rabble, and they were facing a much larger body of well trained, well equipped, highly experienced soldiers.

In such a desperate situation if Bruce had a significant number of extra men who were capable of taking the field, would he have left them behind to mind the pots and pans? That's an awful lot of kitchen help. For each group of ten soldiers, it would allow for a head chef, sous chef, commis chef and a chef de partie and still leave one man to do all the washing up. This seems pretty unlikely in an army that prided itself on being able to march on a diet of oat cakes.

The second problem is that the English army of the day was the most feared fighting machine in Europe. Its ranks included battle-scarred veterans of conflicts in France and even farther abroad. In addition, England's relative prosperity gave it a much better provisioned army than the Scots. Are we to believe that such a force would have been fazed by the appearance of even fifteen thousand peasants armed with cooking pots and wooden sticks? The English would more likely have welcomed the sight as an indication that the Scots were scraping the bottom of the barrel and were on the verge of a complete collapse.

Of course, Barbour's numbers are almost certainly exaggerated. But if we reduce the number of camp followers to cope with the first problem, we increase the significance of the second.

Most historians have tried to cope with this difficulty by suggesting that neither the size nor the impact of the camp followers was as great as Barbour claims. But this approach causes a third problem. What was it that turned the day for the Scots if it wasn't that bunch of "small folk?"

A Legend Lost and Found

Fortunately, there is an explanation that fits the known facts very well, and the fact that Barbour ignores it actually renders it all the more convincing. Given eyewitness reports from both armies, it is clear that Bruce had reserves close at hand, possibly hidden behind Coxet Hill, about a quarter of a mile away. But these reserves were not an ill-disciplined rabble, and they didn't number anywhere near 15,000 men. If there were any ordinary infantrymen in the unit, they took their orders from a small group of knights at its head, knights whose bearded, shaven-headed appearance made them instantly recognizable as crack fighting men whose sudden appearance on the field would make any enemy waver. And what they hoisted wasn't a bed sheet, but instead the white banner under which they had ridden forth many times in the Holy Land. For, according to this explanation, it was the Knights Templar who finally decided the battle of Bannockburn.

This might seem a rather grand claim, but it's one which modern historians are treating more and more seriously. In Scotland, the story of Bannockburn has always come with an optional Templar legend attached, and a convincing body of evidence – though mostly circumstantial – is now leading people elsewhere to believe that the legend may in fact be the true version of the story.

Ironically, the first piece of evidence is Barbour's unlikely story of the fighting bottle washers. This story's lack of credibility suggests that it was used to cover up what really happened that day. But the reason Barbour felt the need for a cover story is a story in itself.

Barbour's account of the battle appears in his epic poem, *The Brus*, which was written in about 1375 to rouse support for the faltering kingship of Robert II. This Robert was Robert Bruce's grandson, and Barbour got the job partly because he was an Archdeacon of the established church and therefore a good choice to lead a major public relations effort.

In this situation, what Barbour needed to produce was a nationalistic clarion call that would gain support for the king. What he didn't need to produce was a story that would land his country in fresh trouble with the pope by praising the Templars, who were still regarded in Church circles as convicted heretics.

We say "fresh trouble" because Bruce had managed to get himself in trouble with the Church several years earlier. And that is the second piece of evidence linking Bannockburn with the Templars. In fact, it's the starting point of a story that links the decline and fall of the Knights Templar with the rise of Robert Bruce's star.

In 1306 Bruce was trying to position himself as Scotland's head of state, but he wasn't having much success. Part of his problem was that Scotland had lost its identity. It was still struggling to drive out the occupying English and at the same time reclaim national status for itself. The other main hitch was that Bruce wasn't the only one seeking the job. The Scots had always been a divided people, and there were several regional leaders who wanted to be king.

Bruce solved part of the problem by killing his main rival, but unfortunately the incident occurred in a church. It was probably unpremeditated – one of those medieval shoving matches that seemed to occur almost spontaneously – but it was enough to get Bruce on the wrong side of the religious establishment back in Rome. He was promptly excommunicated, which in the medieval world was a virtual kiss of death, especially for anyone who aspired to be a head of state.

Bruce reacted quickly and took the desperate gamble of having himself proclaimed King of Scots in the wake of his rival's death. That might have succeeded, but the subsequent loss of the battle of Methven scattered his supporters, which in turn made Bruce a fugitive in his own land as well as a target of the English.

In late 1307 he disappeared for a few months, seeking support in unknown quarters. But the disappearance was not a panicked retreat. Bruce left his wife and daughter with friends and, according to rumor, slipped away to Ireland to negotiate for the help he needed to get his career back on track.

Meanwhile, the Knights Templar were running into trouble of their own. They had fought valiantly in the Crusades, and as the Crusades wound down, the Templars fought in engagements closer to home. (In 1298, they even rode against William Wallace at the battle of Falkirk.) But on Friday the 13th of October, 1307 they, like Robert Bruce, became outlaws in need of a refuge. On that date Philip IV of France staged a series of dawn raids on Templar preceptories throughout France.

The Templars, never without friends in high places, seem to have known of the raids in advance and had time to arrange for several of their high-ranking officials to vanish, along with an unspecified amount of Templar treasure. But that didn't solve the basic problem.

Although a few countries, such as Spain, offered limited help by creating new military Orders for the fugitives to blend into, the Templars must have seen the writing on the wall. If they didn't, the king helped clarify the issue.

Philip enlisted the aid of the Church, and he and Pope Clement set out on a campaign to bring the full weight of both civil and ecclesiastical law to bear. During the next few years, individual Templars were tortured to extract confessions, and several were burned at the stake. Meanwhile, the wheels of justice ground on until it became obvious that the king was eventually going to get whatever verdict he wanted.

At that point, the Templars could not hope to operate in France or Italy. Their only refuge was in more remote countries, where the French king had little influence. And among those countries was Scotland, where an ongoing war had disrupted normal procedures and the "king" had recently been excommunicated. There, even papal authority had little force.

Scotland may seem a strange place for the Templars to seek refuge, but in fact it was far from a strange land. The Order had connections with that country reaching back to just after their inception.

A French knight named Hugh de Payens founded the Templars in 1118, and one of his first official acts was to tour Europe in search of support for his fledgling organization. He achieved considerable success, and from his letters to wavering colleagues in the Holy Land, his success came none too soon. In fact, it appears that Hugh's mission was an absolute necessity. In their early years the Order was so short of men and money that they would certainly have failed if they hadn't received support from Christian Europe.

A Congenial Kingdom

Nowhere did the Templars get a more sympathetic hearing than in Scotland. And at the time, Scotland needed help of its own.

For some years that part of the world had been receiving capable leadership from Malcolm Canmore and his wife, the saintly Margaret. The couple had done much to transform the rough and ready collection of peoples who lived in the Scottish lowlands into a nation capable of looking after itself. But the Scots were an independent lot, and the concept of modern nationhood had yet to develop in the West. As a result, even Malcolm and Margaret could not quite pull the people together.

In their turn, several of Malcolm and Margaret's sons ruled the kingdom, concluding with a power-sharing agreement that lasted from around 1113 until 1124, when the youngest son, David, assumed the throne in his own right.

David quite literally inherited a divided kingdom, but he continued the nation building process begun by his parents. Recognizing that the key to Scotland's survival was stability and a sound economic base, he accelerated the development of a Norman-style feudal system and encouraged the immigration of Norman nobles to operate it. Curiously, however, many of the "Norman" families he invited to move in weren't from Normandy, but from Flanders, a coastal region that lay to the north of Normandy and in many ways was more closely associated with the Low Countries than with France.

David instituted a policy of deliberately settling Flemish traders in the Forth and Clyde valleys, and his decision had an immediate effect on the area's development. New towns sprang up, dedicated to ferrying Scottish raw materials – mostly wool and hides – across the Channel and bringing back finished goods.

The influence of those plantations of Flemish families can still be seen in the architecture of villages in such places as Fife's East Neuk. Pan tiled roofs and crow stepped gables huddle near the Forth estuary and narrow cobbled streets lead to the all-important harbor, making parts of the town look for all the world like a traditional Flemish village.

Grants of land to various monastic Orders – especially the Cistercians, who in later years were the Templars' spiritual partners – was another part of the process. The incoming French and English abbots built cathedral communities which were far more efficient in their use of land and resources than their secular neighbors. Monastic Orders were soon at the forefront of the wool exporting business, and their farming methods were years ahead of those traditionally used by Scottish peasants. As a result, everybody in Scotland went up a learning curve, and everybody began to profit from the new system.

By the time Hugh de Payens came seeking an audience, this process was well under way, and it was only logical for the king to give generous grants of land to the fledgling Templars. But it seems that David was genuinely pious as well. Contemporary reports indicate that he soon had a bodyguard of Templars, who were supposedly guardians of his morals as well as his person.

Thus the Templars managed to form a strong connection with the Scottish nobility, and over the next few centuries both sides diligently cultivated their links with the other. This situation wasn't hurt by the fact that De Payens had married a member of the St. Clair family. The St. Clairs were a French family, but they had a Scottish branch that became extremely prominent in the Lowlands and was also to become inextricably linked over the centuries with both the Templars and the Freemasons.

With connections like these, the Templars forged strong links with Scotland, especially in the Forth-Clyde valley, where Robert Bruce later rose to power. Many members of the Scottish upper classes took the cross and fought side by side with the Templars in the Holy Land, and some even took the Order's vows and became full fledged members.

In time, the Knights Templar came to own around five hundred properties in Scotland, making them one of the country's most influential forces. That's why the fugitive Templars of the early 1300's found the country a logical place to seek refuge. That, in turn, changed the nature of the Templars' presence in Scotland and set the stage for their dealings with Robert Bruce.

During the early parts of his career, Bruce gained support from such key noble families as the Setons and the St. Clairs, who were later known as Sinclairs. Both families had Templar connections, so it would be remarkable if someone hadn't suggested that the king-in-search-of-an-army have a few words with the knights-in-search-of-a-safe-haven. In modern management parlance, this was going to be a win-win negotiation.

But as it turns out, the Templars were in a position to supply the fugitive king with more than just a few wily old soldiers. By 1312 England's Edward II was complaining that Irish "merchants" were supplying the Scots with weapons – an odd claim, given that the Irish were too poor to have an arms industry. On the other hand, the Templars had a number of preceptories on the west coast of Ireland, an area that was technically under English control but was so remote that it was difficult to keep tabs on.

Immediately after the Templars were raided in 1307, their fleet supposedly put to sea from La Rochelle, in south-west France. The fleet could have carried its men and munitions anywhere, but there are no records that the Templar ships were ever seen again. Apparently they went to some out of the way place. And in those days the west coast of Ireland was as out of the way as any place.

Of course, we can only speculate about the fate of the Templar fleet and the source of the arms the Irish were supposedly selling to the Scots. But we must remember that the Templars suddenly became fugitives in late 1307, about the same time Robert Bruce dropped out of sight for a few months. Bruce reportedly went to Ireland to seek help in his troubled campaign against the English. The Templars had men and materials in Ireland. Their fleet disappeared with all its men and armaments aboard. And within a few years the English king was complaining that the Scots were being supplied with weapons from Ireland.

It's almost as if something clandestine was going on. But is there any evidence?

At this point perhaps we should pause to take another look at the ritual of the Royal Order of Scotland. We have observed that the ritual says the Order was established on Mt. Moriah (the temple mount in Jerusalem where the Templars actually had their headquarters) and later re-established at Kilwinning, where the king of Scotland presided over the group. The king in question, of course, was Robert Bruce.

We concluded that the reference to Kilwinning was partly intended to give the story the prestige of great age, but that it also seemed to point to some actual bit of history. Here we may have that bit of history.

If Bruce really did strike a deal with the Templars, their first move would have been to transfer arms and men from Ireland to Scotland, and their most likely route was across the Irish Sea and south-western Scotland. During the few months he was out of sight, Bruce would probably have spent time in both Ireland and the west of Scotland organizing the operation. But precisely where would he and the Templars have met to do it?

During this period of history, the Templars were known to operate in Argyll, which consisted of the middle section of western Scotland, so they knew the area well and undoubtedly had friends who could help them arrange meetings. But under the circumstances they had special requirements. They needed an isolated spot, preferably near the coast and under the jurisdiction of sympathetic Scots who could guarantee security and privacy.

Kilwinning certainly met these conditions. It was off the beaten track, nestled in rolling hills a good distance south-west of Glasgow and less than ten miles from the coast. And the abbey that had long stood at Kilwinning could offer the protection of sympathetic members of the Scottish religious establishment. All in all, it wasn't a bad place for a secret meeting, but it wasn't the only place that fitted the bill.

In this regard, the Royal Order's ritual offers an enticing snippet that is almost always ignored but crystallizes this part of the legend into an almost tangible piece of evidence. The ritual makes passing reference to a place called Icolmkill. Specifically, it tells us that the Royal Order was re-established at Icolmkill before it met at Kilwinning.

This is certainly a curious detail. The ritual makes nothing more of the claim, and even long time members of the Order have no idea where or what Icolmkill is ... or was. In fact, until now it hasn't found a place in our investigation. But at this point it suddenly becomes a key element in the story.

Icolmkill was the ancient Scottish name for the island of Iona. This small island is part of the Inner Hebrides. It's just off the western coast of Scotland and almost touches the south-western tip of the larger island of Mull.

Iona is easily accessible from Ireland and partly for that reason was St. Columba's first landfall in his mission to convert the Scottish people to Christianity. Columba established the Celtic Church there, and that Church had a number of disputes with Rome over the centuries.

Templars fleeing Europe during those last terrible days of their Order's downfall would have found the island a very congenial place. Like Kilwinning, it was relatively isolated but easy to reach from their preceptories in Ireland. It was the site of an old monastery tied to a Church that still saw itself as more Celtic than Roman. And it was a point of entry to the Scottish mainland, where the Templars and their arms were badly needed.

For Bruce's part, Iona and Kilwinning provided the quickest and easiest access to Ireland. Scotland is at its narrowest there, and the lowland terrain made travel relatively easy, while the area was remote enough to avoid the prying eyes of the English.

In this light, it appears that the Royal Order's legend presents a very credible, though heavily veiled description of conditions that existed during the years that led up to Bannockburn. When Bruce and the Templars realized they needed each other, it would have made perfect sense for them to hold an initial meeting on Iona. After reaching an agreement there, they would likely have met again in Ireland and Kilwinning to organize their operations, to supervise the transportation of much needed arms from Templar store rooms in Ireland ... and to assemble the small group of Templar knights who would train and advise Bruce's ragtag army.

As we look more closely at the Royal Order's legend, it does seem that all the pieces fit together. What at first appeared to be just another fraternal legend now looks like a story of actual events, composed by people who knew the real story. And that story seems to tell what actually happened during those few months when Robert Bruce was desperately trying to salvage his career.

Immediately after those crucial months in the fall of 1307, Robert Bruce's fortunes did indeed improve dramatically. In military terms, he seemed to grow up fast, and in particular his tactics got smarter. Instead of full frontal assaults against the English, he now organized raids carried out by troops of fast, lightly armed horsemen. This was the same tactic used by the Saracens in the Holy Land. And castles were now taken by subterfuge instead of siege, often by using rope ladders to scale their walls at night. That was another Moslem trick.

Little by little, Bruce was winning the war, and he was using tactics that were little known in the West but quite common in the East. In other words, Robert Bruce was suddenly using methods known by few people other than the Templars.

In the meantime, the Order of the Temple was losing what little support it had left. Even in England, where Edward II had done everything he could to resist Philip and Clement's efforts, Templars were now being rounded up and imprisoned. Edward reluctantly allowed French torturers to come to England to extract confessions from them, and with the moral ambiguity for which he was famous, he simultaneously stripped Templar estates of their assets to pay for his war against the Scots.

By 1312 the Templars had officially ceased to exist. Papal bulls excommunicated the Order and transferred all their remaining assets to the Knights Hospitaller, a similar military Order of monks who had managed to keep their noses clean with the authorities. But in the slow moving world of the Middle Ages, the matter dragged on a little longer.

It was not until March 1314 that the last recorded act of the Templars' long and dramatic history was played out. Four of the Order's surviving leaders, including its Grand Master, Jacques de Molay, refused to confirm confessions extracted from them under torture. That robbed the French king of a satisfactory conclusion to his campaign against the Order, and he reacted by having the four burned at the stake in Paris. Now there was no way back for any Templars who remained at large, and it was just three months before the battle of Bannockburn.

Historians have long toyed with the idea that at least some of the Templars did go underground. There are theories that they survived on the north-western fringes of Europe and Scotland. And a few extreme theories even have them traveling to America.

There may be a grain of truth in all of these stories. The Templars were in fact an international organization with branches everywhere. Many of their members did in fact retire or join other monastic groups. But many of today's organizations claim descent from fugitive Templars, and some have pedigrees that lend credibility to their claims. So it is worth exploring the notion that the Royal Order of Scotland does in fact have historic ties with the medieval Knights Templar.

The Templars certainly would have found Scotland a congenial kingdom in which to operate during their final days, not to mention a suitable place for a last refuge. Politically, they might have found it difficult to support the excommunicated Robert Bruce. But when they themselves came under threat of torture, excommunication and dissolution, that dilemma must have seemed much less significant. After all, Bruce's father and grandfather had fought alongside the crusading armies in the Holy Land, and with the wind blowing against the Templars even in England, they had little to lose by being friendly to the Scots. Casting their lot with Bruce was a risky strategy, but one of the few options they had left.

There is every reason to believe that the Templars did indeed take that option, and that it had results neither they nor Bruce could have anticipated.

Sterling Castle

Knighthoods and Anonymity

According to some reports, the Scots army drilled for months in the Torwood, near Falkirk, in preparation for Bannockburn. If it was the Templars who supervised the drilling, they did a good job, as demonstrated by a skirmish on the eve of the main battle. A division of five hundred Scottish infantry, fighting in close formation, drove off eight hundred English cavalry.

These are Barbour's numbers and are probably inflated. Still, they describe quite an impressive action, and one that could not have been achieved by the ill-disciplined amalgamation of clansmen the Scottish army was supposed to be. Facing a hail of deadly missiles from the English horsemen, the Scots seem to have maintained their composure and held their ranks in the face of unfavorable odds. Unable to break through the wall of Scots pikes, and suffering heavy casualties, the English force finally broke off, abandoning their plan of flanking the Scottish army and reaching their goal, the strategically located Stirling Castle.

Another clue that the Templars had a hand in the battle comes from one of the English chroniclers. In his account of the battle, Thomas Gray makes passing reference to the defection of an English knight called Alexander de Seton to the Scots camp.

Now, at first glance a minor incident of this sort might seem trivial, especially since Gray is the only one who says anything about it. But there's something intriguing about this particular footnote to history.

Sir Thomas Gray of Heton wrote his version of the Bannockburn story in the 1350's, not long after the events actually occurred. And while he was the only one to mention Seton's defection, his account has serious credibility. His father, also called Sir Thomas Gray of Heton, was a participant in the action. The elder Thomas was on the English side and was captured on the 23rd. This placed him in the Scottish camp as a prisoner on the day of the battle. But he wasn't an ordinary captive. As a prisoner of rank, he was given the courtesies due a gentleman. And that may well have placed him in a position to overhear any discussion between Seton and the Scottish leadership on the eve of the battle.

What Seton had to say on that occasion is important because Alexander de Seton belonged to a Scottish family with Templar connections, and modern writers suspect he was in fact a Templar agent gathering information on behalf of the Scots. Whether this supposition is true or not, Seton did bring important information on English deployments and numbers, thus giving the Scots an opportunity to make last minute adjustments to their battle plan. In fact, it is just possible that Seton's information gave Scottish tacticians the idea that a properly coordinated charge by reserves would win the day.

The rest, as they say, is history. The next morning, Bruce put a shrewd plan into action, a mysterious force appeared at a crucial moment, and the English were routed. The only thing that stopped the Scots from finishing the job by capturing Edward was their reluctance to send a sufficient force to chase after him. But this, too, may be a clue that Templars were directing the battle. Most Scots, being an aggressive people, would have chased a retreating enemy, but the Templars had seen too many feigned withdrawals in the Holy Land to risk falling for that Saracen-style trick.

Taken one at a time, these clues may be tenuous, but together they lead to the conclusion that the last remnants of the Knights Templar did indeed take the Scottish side in the final years of the Wars of Independence. That's certainly a romantic picture. The few remaining knights of a once venerated Order, seen by many – both then and now – as the living embodiment of the Grail romances, gathered in a Scottish field for one last battle. Men who might have been novices at the fall of Acre, when the Crusaders were pushed out of the Holy Land some years earlier, now stirred their aging limbs to fight for the freedom of a country at the edge of the world. And through their efforts, they handed their ally a crown that was once worn by their old friend, David I.

In return, these valiant knights received refuge from the papal inquisitors who still threatened them. And if we are to believe the legend of the Royal

Order of Scotland, they were also granted a new Order of knighthood to replace the one stripped from them by their temporal and spiritual masters in Europe.

But if the Royal Order's legend is a true account of this historic incident, what are we to make of its claim that "masons" were knighted *after* the battle? On mediaeval battlefields, knighthoods were generally handed out before the main event.

This was the standard practice for prosaic reasons. A knighthood was not simply a fancy title that allowed a country squire to lord it over his neighbors. It usually came with grants of land and property, which benefited not only the new knight but his family as well. When a young warrior was knighted before the battle, he at least knew that his family would receive an estate if he died that day.

Besides, knighthoods were granted as much for supporting the king's cause as for performing feats of prowess. Just by showing up at the battle site, a fighter demonstrated his willingness to put his life on the line, and that in itself was a reason to reward him. It wasn't just services previously rendered but services about to be rendered that the king was recognizing by granting honors before a battle.

On the morning of the battle of Bannockburn, Robert Bruce followed the traditional forms assiduously. After hearing mass and having "a slight meal" (no need for complicated food preparation there), the army got into formation and, according to Barbour, "they made knights, as the custom is among those of the craft of war." Bruce knighted James Douglas and Walter Stewart, two of his trusted lieutenants. Then the army marched forward and were shrived for battle by priests bearing St. Columba's relics in an ark-shaped container which still survives and is now known as the Monymusk reliquary.

The fact that they did all this in the full sight of the English army is shown by Barbour's description of the scene. Edward II is supposed to have said, "What, will these Scots fight?"

Sir Ingram de Umfraville, an English knight long experienced in fighting the Scots, told Edward he was sure these men would indeed fight. Moreover, he said, they were the finest sight he had ever seen, "Scotsmen undertaking to fight against the great might of England." He was so impressed, in fact, that he advised Edward to make a feigned withdrawal to break the Scottish ranks.

But Edward would have none of it. He had come to have a straight up battle, and that's how it would be.

Just then, the Scots knelt to take the benediction from the priests. "Look," said the English king, "They kneel for mercy!"

Once again De Umfraville was keen to put the king right. He explained that the Scots were yielding to a higher authority than Edward: "Yonder men will win all or die. None there shall flee for fear of death."

What this shows, apart from Ingram de Umfraville's lack of tact, is that the knighthoods Bruce handed out took place as part of the standard prebattle ceremonial. But we have seen that many of Bruce's men were not yet present on the field of battle. They were the ones who charged over the hill late that afternoon and took away the English army's last hope of victory. Of all those present on this occasion, they were certainly the ones most deserving of a reward.

Those men apparently missed the ceremonial in which Bruce bestowed knighthoods before the battle, and the official record says nothing about honors being handed out afterward. But it would be an ungrateful king who did not reward the men who gave him his greatest victory, especial if those men were ex-Templars who had been supplying and advising the Scottish army during its glory days.

There were probably only a few Templars on the field, perhaps fifty or sixty. They had always been a small, elite group, and as fugitives we would expect no more than a handful to be fighting with the Scottish army. The

Royal Order claims sixty-three were knighted, and that may be as good a guess as any.

The handing out of knighthoods after the battle and the number of men involved are minor details, and at first blush they do seem historically inaccurate. But it is now clear that they actually give an air of truth to the Royal Order's legend, which may in fact be the truest account of the battle that has survived. The Scots advanced, the English lost ground and then reformed, and a small group of Templars charged out from behind a hill to settle the issue. Then, while most of Bruce's troops were passing over the dead, he took time to reward his allies for their crucial help. He created a new Order of knighthood, as the ritual says, honoring sixty-three men – Templars, not masons – for the service they had performed. And at the end of the day a few good men departed the battlefield with their heads held high.

A legend was born on that 24th of June. It was passed down through the centuries by Scottish families of noble blood, families whose members had actually participated in their country's greatest battle. And the Templars who won the battle? They withdrew to enjoy their victory and perpetuated its story in the legend of the new Order the king had created for them.

Preserving the Legend

Before we leave the story, there is an interesting postscript to the battle of Bannockburn, and it comes from an unexpected source. We have seen that the Premier Grand Lodge of England adopted a revised version of the *Old Constitutions* to serve as their book of constitutions. But they didn't do it right away. In fact, they waited more than five years after they were established to appoint the Scottish minister, James Anderson, to write their constitutions for them.

If the Grand Lodge had been eager to have a set of constitutions drawn up, they certainly would have acted more quickly. The long delay suggests that they were in no hurry for such a document, and they may not have felt they needed one at all.

This confirms the view of many scholars that it was not the Grand Lodge but James Anderson who was pushing the idea of adapting the *Old Constitutions* for use by the newly formed Masonic body. He apparently wanted to be sure Freemasonry included this ancient document as part of its official makeup. But what was it about the *Old Constitutions* that made it important?

Since most of the commotion during the Grand Lodge's early years had to do with tradition and the basic nature of Freemasonry, we can reasonably guess that's what Dr. Anderson was concerned about. Apparently the *Old Constitutions* contained something which defined Masonry as it existed in the old days, and he wanted to be sure the Grand Lodge didn't lose track of it.

The document contained a legendary history of Masonry tracing it back to Adam, but even in the eighteenth century the Masons must have regarded such a pedigree as largely fictitious, or at least as something to be taken with a large grain of salt.

There was also a set of charges traditionally given to new members during the medieval period, but the lodges of the eighteenth century had already gone beyond the old charges. They now had their own set of initiation ceremonies. To be sure, the new rituals were based on ancient ceremonies. But the Grand Lodge wasn't about to abandon them and go back to something which was seriously out of date. Most likely Dr. Anderson wasn't interested in any of this. He was concerned with the part of the document that went to the heart of the organization's past – a story called the York Legend.

The York Legend says that King Athelstan re-introduced the craft of stone masonry to England. But he found problems with the craft, so he reorganized it and established a new set of regulations to govern it. The resulting organization was what, according to the Masonic lodges who carefully preserved the *Old Constitutions*, evolved into the modern Craft of Freemasonry.

But this story doesn't quite hold water. The craft of stone masonry was firmly established in England by the time Athelstan became king in A.D. 925. So he could not have been the one who re-introduced it to the island.

Stone architecture was originally introduced to Britain by the Romans, beginning in the first century A.D. The ancient Britons had built mostly with wood, and it wasn't until the Romans arrived that any significant work was done in stone. Then, when the Romans pulled out in the fifth century, the Britons reverted to using wood and thatch construction. Those materials were also favored by the Anglo-Saxons, who moved in to replace the Romans. As a result, stone architecture was largely abandoned in the island, though only for a few centuries.

Building in stone was in fact re-introduced during the seventh and eighth centuries as part of a revival of Anglo-Saxon arts and crafts. But all of this occurred at least two centuries before Athelstan's time. When he became king, the craft was quite common in England.

So it appears that the York Legend really is legend rather than history. Still, that doesn't mean it's complete fiction. Most legends are based on some bit of real history. And given the context in which we find it, the history which formed the basis for the York Legend is presumably the true story of Freemasonry's origin. This must be the part of the *Old Constitutions* James Anderson was trying to insert in the Grand Lodge's official documents.

But after so many years how can we uncover the real history behind the York Legend? The first thing to remember is that James Anderson came from Scotland. And since all the dissident Grand Lodges, except of course the York Grand Lodge, had some connection with Scotland, it's reasonable to assume that the history we're looking for had something to do with that country.

If so, it would tie everything together. Although we don't know precisely what ritual the York Grand Lodge used, it probably drew heavily from the material in the *Old Constitutions*. It was the most prominent Masonic document known, and it was as available to Masons in York as anywhere else. Besides, the Masons of Yorkshire couldn't help being attracted to a legend that traced the beginnings of modern Freemasonry to their own city of York.

If York's ritual did in fact contain a veiled account of something that came out of Scotland, then even the York Grand Lodge was trying to go back to the Fraternity's Scottish roots. But we still haven't seen what it is about the York Legend that points to Scotland. To resolve this mystery, we need to extract the basic story from the York Legend and see how it compares with Scottish history.

For the moment we'll forget that the story is about Athelstan and a group of imported stone masons. Those details may have been added at a later date to conceal the real actors in this curious play.

If we remove all the particulars and details from the legend, the bare bones that remain tell a simple story. A British king imported a group of skilled men. He realized there were problems with the organization to which they belonged, so he reorganized them and gave them a new set of regulations. And the resulting organization evolved into modern Masonry.

But when did this happen? Since the story claims to be history and not prophesy, we can be sure it occurred before the legend was committed to paper. The oldest surviving copy of the *Old Constitutions* is called the Regius Poem. It was written about 1390, but linguists who have studied the text say it was probably composed half a century earlier and shows signs of being written by someone in England (possibly in the West Midlands, according to some linguistic experts). So we are looking for an incident in Scottish history that happened before the middle of the fourteenth century and was chronicled by someone from England.

We can also establish a starting date for our inquiry. Since the king we are looking for is presumably a king of Scotland, we should not go farther back than the first king of Scots, Kenneth Mac Alpin who was crowned in 844. Therefore we are looking for something that happened between 844 and about 1350. This is a span of five centuries, but we may be able to narrow our search even more.

Freemasonry has always claimed a connection with gothic architecture. The bulk of its symbols, including the famous "working tools," are linked with the construction of cathedrals. And the Craft's actual history, so far as we can reconstruct it, has the Fraternity evolving from lodges which arose specifically to aid the traveling masons who built those cathedrals.

Since the construction of gothic cathedrals began in the twelfth century, it makes sense to assume that the history we're looking for occurred after that time. Of course, legends often combine episodes from several periods of history and present them as if they all occurred at one time. In this case, the legend seems to have combined material pointing to the actual re-introduction of stone masonry in the seventh century with other material pointing to something that happened much later. So we should not expect to find the whole story of Masonic origins in the years between the beginning of gothic architecture and the writing of the Regius Poem. But since we know that we are dealing with both a Scottish King and the stone masons, it's the most logical place to start.

Our search, then, boils down to a period beginning in the twelfth century and ending in the middle of the fourteenth. It has to do with a British – probably Scottish – king and a group of imported men who had skills that were not already available in the island. And it involves the reorganization of their group.

When we put all the pieces together, one episode stands out. At the beginning of the fourteenth century the Knights Templar were put on trial for their lives. This occurred in France, but the Templars were an international organization. And they were tried by the Church, which was also international. So the proceedings did not stay inside the borders of France for long.

When the Templars were arrested in France on October 13, 1307, the pope demanded that England's King Edward II arrest the Templars in his country, too. But Edward was on good terms with the Order. He dragged his feet and made no arrests until late December, giving the English Templars time to escape.

Though the Templars left no records of their flight, historians have always believed that they fled northward to Yorkshire and southern Scotland. It was in those parts that the Order owned large tracts of land and had business contacts and friends who could help them.

Our picture of Masonic origins is now beginning to develop, and we can start to see some details. The earliest version of the York Legend may well have been written by a Templar scribe from southern or midland England who fled northward with his brothers. And the Templars who reached southern Scotland? According to legend, they were the ones who saved the day at Bannockburn a mere seven years later.

Seen in this light, the story told by the York Legend is essentially the same as the story told by the ritual of the Royal Order of Scotland. Robert Bruce, the king of Scotland, imported a group of skilled men. They were the fugitive Templars, who are called masons in the Royal Order's ritual as well as in the York Legend. As an outlawed Order which had been suppressed by the Church, the Templars certainly had problems. They needed to be reorganized in some way. So Bruce rewarded them for their assistance not by granting them land or money but by creating a new Order of knighthood for them. And that Order became the Masons.

It appears that all the Masonic roads lead to Bannockburn.

Anderson's contribution was the *Old Constitutions* and its York Legend, which may also have been reflected in the ritual of the York Grand Lodge. That ritual, though now lost, was claimed to be the oldest and purest form of Masonry. Certainly this would be a reasonable claim for anyone whose ritual was based on a Masonic document that came straight from the

Middle Ages. If the York working was indeed a reflection of this legend, then all the dissident Grand Lodges, without exception, were pointing to Scotland.

Just a few years after the Craft adopted Anderson's *Constitutions*, a Templar tradition was introduced to Freemasonry by Andrew Michael Ramsay. He was a Scotsman and a supporter of the Stewart dynasty, which was founded by Robert Bruce's daughter. Ramsay introduced the Chivalric tradition in France, the original home of the Templars, where Bonnie Prince Charlie was exiled at the time, and where the idea that Templars became Masons would most likely be accepted.

And what happened when the mainstream of Freemasonry insisted on moving away from this tradition? The Royal Order of Scotland stepped in and carried the torch, preserving the claim that Masonry was created at Bannockburn.

It is beginning to look as if the Templar tradition is more than legend. Several strands of evidence have brought us to the conclusion that fugitive Templars became involved in Scottish affairs. They took on a new identity, and their organization eventually became the modern Craft.

We have finally located the origin of Freemasonry as an organization, but something is missing. We have not yet found the origin of its ritual. Could this mean that we have somehow gone astray?

Actually, the answer is quite simple. In this most curious fraternity, it is a fact that the ritual predates the organization. And the proof rests on clues that will take us to the home of the Templars and to a minstrel whose name is barely remembered today but whose work is known by almost everyone.

Borestone Memorial, Bannockburn

The spot where Bruce traditionally planted his standard
on 24 June, 1314, before advancing on the English.

CHAPTER 4

THE HOLY GRAIL AND THE LODGE

How It All Began

WE have seen how the Templars became associated with the Masons and how they contributed to Masonic legends. But there is another legend about the medieval Templars which explains how the very first Masonic ritual was born. This is the legend that the Templars were somehow involved with the Holy Grail, and it got its start with the first of the Grail stories.

In the closing years of the twelfth century, a man named Chretien de Troyes wrote the earliest known version of the Grail legend in a poem titled *Conte del Graal*. He claimed that it was based on "the best story that has ever been told in royal court" and that the story came from a book he received from Count Philip of Flanders. Philip asked Chretien to write a new version of the story, and the result was nine thousand lines of poetry including the adventures of a knight named Perceval and his adventures with the Holy Grail.

At first blush all of this seems plain enough, but when we take a closer look at the poem and the circumstances that surround it, we encounter yet another set of riddles. To begin with, Chretien's claim that he wrote the poem at the request of a patron is a little curious. It isn't that working for a patron was unusual. In fact, this was the way most artists earned a living in those days. It was certainly standard procedure for writers, and Chretien routinely followed the practice; he states, for example, that Countess Marie of Champagne gave him both the plot and the allegory for his poem, *Lancelot*.

The problem is that the book Philip supposedly gave to Chretien hasn't been identified. Although scholars have searched for centuries, they could never pin down Chretien's source, and this leaves us to wonder if there ever was such a book.

At this point we must be very precise in understanding the problem. It isn't that Chretien would have objected to copying someone else's story. In the twelfth century there was no such thing as copyright law, and everyone copied from everyone else.

Chretien de Troyes was no exception. He worked in the tradition of the Breton minstrels, who developed the Arthurian romances. These minstrels told stories to entertain their hosts, and they drew from a long list of traditional tales, making changes from time to time as they saw fit. As Chretien well knew, the Arthurian romances were among those traditional tales. So, as he freely admits, he wasn't trying to write a completely new story.

In addition, the Arthurian tales weren't even French in origin. They were Celtic, meaning largely Irish and Welsh, but with the Scots having their own versions.

The Source of Arthur's Legend

In fact, the Grail legends, the Templars, and Scotland are all bound together. We have seen that there were active trade routes between Flanders and Scotland as early as the time of David I. One of the commodities that regularly crossed the seas was Scottish culture, twelfth century style. So it is no coincidence that the Grail legends which began to circulate among the court poets of Flanders had a distinctly Celtic tinge. Scotland had its own share of home grown Arthurian romances, along with legends that named local places as the likely sites of the "real" Camelot. Some of the original stories may have been imported to the continent by Irish or Welsh sea-captains, but they are just as likely to have come from the Flemish Scots who traded with their cousins back home. It is no surprise, then, that when Chretien came to write his masterpiece in the 1180's – a mere generation after the end of David's reign – he had many Scottish versions of the old Celtic sources to draw on.

Of course, Scotland wasn't the only source of these legends, just as it wasn't the only place where the Templars had a special relationship with the nobility. Indeed, the English as well as the Scots went to great pains to present themselves as the true inheritors of the Arthurian mantle and, by implication, as crusading soul mates of the Templars.

A little more than a century after Chretien's time, the fruits of this effort were highly visible throughout the island. In 1301, Edward I had his son, the future Edward II, invested as Prince of Wales. But he didn't use an ordinary "royal" ceremony. Instead, the proceedings were held in the plush surroundings of the Templars' English headquarters, known as the London Temple. And by all accounts they were deliberately planned with echoes of Arthur and his knights in mind. A few years later, when Edward I lay dying, the Scots unearthed a prophecy, supposedly uttered by Merlin himself. It said that when Edward ("Le Roi Coveytous") died, the Celtic people of Britain would rise up and shake off the chains that bound them. Robert Bruce drew from Arthurian lore, too, consistently presenting himself as the gentle perfect knight. While he was a fugitive, he was known to cheer up his followers by reading them a romance called *Fierebras*. And as we have seen, Bruce's final act was to ask that his heart be taken on crusade by his trusted lieutenants – a gesture Arthur himself might have been proud of.

Chretien got much of his material from the stories that came out of this same tradition, and he would have had no problem writing a poem based on a book someone had shown him. But since scholars have never been able to pin down the elusive "book" he supposedly used as a basis for *Conte del*

Graal, we are at something of a loss in deciding where the material came from. And that, in a nutshell, is the next puzzle we have to solve.

Another Hidden Agenda?

It is obvious that much of the poem's contents are from the old Celtic myths. The similarities are unmistakable. But what isn't obvious is whether Chretien used that material to create a more lyrical version of an old story or used bits and pieces of folklore and history to construct something new and different.

Either way, we find ourselves facing the same problem. The peculiar nature of the Grail legend suggests that it contains more than appears on the surface. In fact, parts of the text read like a modern Masonic ritual. They are loaded with symbolism. They contain what scholars often describe (unfairly perhaps) as inconsistencies and absurdities, and they pose an array of questions that are left unanswered. Any answers that are given seem incomplete, and in places the narrative seems more riddle than story.

Many scholars excuse all of this as the result of several generations of retelling and recombining, which occurred before Chretien got hold of the material. Presumably this process left the story fragmented and disjointed. Chretien, we are told, found that his source was a jumble of odds and ends he was unable to repair. So he left the problems in place and simply told the story as he found it.

But this explanation doesn't quite work. Chretien de Troyes was the most important French writer of his century. By the time he wrote the *Graal* he was already famous. He had composed four Arthurian romances, as well as other romances and songs, and he had even translated the Latin poet Ovid, who was very popular in France at the time.

This was a man who knew very well how to handle his source material. Besides, his Grail poem is not a rough draft. Although scholars agree that it was left unfinished, the nine thousand lines we have are well polished. They reflect the talents of a master of his craft at the height of his powers. So we should not believe that he left blatant flaws in a story because he didn't have the skill to correct them.

If he copied someone else's story, it would be strange for him not to edit it to give his own version a clear narrative line. And if he created a new story by putting together bits and pieces of folklore, it would be strange for him to botch his cross weave of the elements he started with.

More likely he made this poem just what he wanted it to be – a curious tale whose difficult passages are carefully placed to demand further thought from the reader. In other words, although *Conte del Graal* as we have it now is unfinished and may well have been due for a few more rounds of fiddling and polishing, we should not doubt that it shows the steady hand of the artist. Instead of treating those difficult passages as mistakes, we should assume that they are just what Chretien intended.

But if the story contains deliberate puzzles and riddles, why should we accept at face value the author's rather lame statement that he liked the story so much he copied it from a book? If that were true, we must believe the story was already widely known. It was not simply a minstrel's tale but one well enough established to have been published – and published in a volume so unremarkable it needed no more comment than that Chretien got it from one of his patrons.

Chretien even fails to give us the title of this book, though he certainly didn't object to naming names. He lists the titles of several of his own works in the opening passages of his historic romance, *Cliges*.

Granted, publishing in those days was done on a much smaller scale than today. But since we have surviving copies of other stories from which Chretien drew, we have to ask why the source of the Grail story is missing.

One possible answer is that *Conte del Graal* was not written as claimed but instead was created for a different reason. If it was, Chretien's statement about his source was obviously intended to hide the truth, and that in itself is a clue that something was afoot.

The Story Behind the Story

Fortunately, the story behind the story is not hard to guess. To learn what was going on behind the scenes, we only have to look at the people who had an interest in the story. And Chretien actually gives us the name of one of those people.

He states that he composed his poem "by command of the count," and the count was Philip of Flanders. So it wasn't the poet who took the first step in creating this story. His patron was the one who brought it to his attention.

This is generally taken at face value: the nobleman was so impressed by a story he had read that he passed it on to a minstrel who might improve it. In those days patrons of the arts often had books written to order, and it could have happened that way. But in this case the "command" may well imply that a wider circle had developed an interest in the story and, for reasons of their own, wanted a version of it tailored to their specific needs.

Once we see the kind of man Philip was, this is not hard to believe. Philip of Flanders (also known as Philip of Alsace) was not just an obscure member of the upper class. He was a very important member of the nobility. He was, in fact, a regent of France and an active participant in the Crusades. Political considerations are never far from the mind of such a man, and even in the twelfth century, books were often used to advance the interests of the people who commissioned them.

We must, therefore, broaden our horizon and consider the circles in which Philip of Flanders and Chretien de Troyes traveled. There we may find clues to a hidden agenda that lay behind the world's first telling of the Grail legend.

Chretien de Troyes lived at a particular moment in history, and we need to look closely at that moment, because any writer's work is influenced by the culture in which he lives and the events unfolding around him. When we look at *Conte del Graal*, we can see that it doesn't just reflect the ramblings of the old Breton minstrels. It's not even connected very closely to the Welsh, Irish and Scottish legends from which much of the Arthurian romances came. Instead, it has more to do with a series of events that had recently unfolded in Chretien's own neighborhood and in a land much farther to the east.

Chretien was born during the early years of the Crusades. And he grew up while the Knights Templar were becoming a powerful force in Europe and, according to persistent legends, were setting out on a quest for sacred relics in the Holy Land.

A connection between Chretien and these events is implied by the fact that he came from the Champagne region of France. This is the same area that spawned Hugh de Payens (the founder of the Templars) and Abbot Bernard of Clairvaux, who revitalized the Cistercian Order and helped the Templars get their start in the world.

It is worth noting that Troyes lies only a few miles north-west of Clairvaux and a similar distance south of Payens, which is on the left bank of the Seine near the point where that river is joined by the Aube.

This bit of geography is important because, although the Templars grew into a major international organization, they were always primarily French. They originated in France, their leadership and much of their rank and file were French, and their last days revolved around political events in that country.

To be more precise, the Templars were organized in Troyes, which places them squarely in Chretien's back yard.

The crucial event was a council held in the cathedral of Troyes on January 13, 1128 and it was no minor affair. Cardinal Matthew of Albano represented the pope. Two archbishops, ten bishops, seven abbots and several members of the nobility also attended.

Abbot Bernard did not preside over the council, mainly because he was in poor health at the time. But he had laid the groundwork for it, and all present knew he was the guiding light of the proceedings. He did manage to show up at the council, though, as did Hugh de Payens, and it was at this event that the Templars gained official status by receiving the blessing of the Church and a Rule of seventy-two articles to govern their affairs.

But even at that early date, there was a hint of the curious role the Templars were to play in the Holy Land. Although their Rule was strict and harsh, it contained a provision allowing the Master to enforce its terms at his discretion. The Order, in other words, began its existence with a measure of independence. And it soon increased its independence by changing its own constitution, eventually adding more than six hundred articles to tailor the document to its particular needs.

Thus the Templars became both a standing army and a religious Order, a new concept in Europe. As they gained strength and wealth, they increasingly asserted their independence until they became a law unto themselves. And all of this began in Troyes.

Now, there is some doubt that Chretien was born and raised in Troyes. Many scholars believe he lived there for only a few years in later life. But those later years are when he wrote the *Graal*, and for us his early life is of little importance. At some point he became so closely associated with the city that he has been identified with it ever since. That in itself tells us he was exposed to the Templars just as they were rising to power, acquiring great wealth and making their plans for the Holy Land.

Of course, just being in the same city doesn't prove that Chretien and the Templars had any direct contact. It only provides the first link in a chain. The rest depends on the way politicians operated in those days.

We don't need to ask if members of the French nobility had hidden agendas. The ambition and intrigue which riddled French politics throughout that era makes it certain that they did. Since France was just beginning to evolve into a nation in the modern sense, it still had a fragmented power structure and suffered from the resulting political struggles. That much is a given. The only question is whether Chretien de Troyes got caught up in one of those hidden agendas and wrote the *Graal* because of it.

Clearly he was in the right place at the right time. As a storyteller he moved freely among the French courts, in part because entertaining the nobility paid better than entertaining the peasants. But once he was exposed to those circles, he gained some of the other benefits of associating with the rich and powerful. Not only did he visit the nobility on a frequent basis, he was there in a social setting as well, and that gave him a great deal of familiarity with them. He was not just a commoner who came to the castle with a petition or some other business; he was close to the inner circle and may actually have been considered a member of the circle.

Nor was this a one sided relationship. As the foremost writer of his day, Chretien had something to offer his hosts. His fluency with the pen would certainly have made him a valuable asset to any nobleman who needed to "get the word out."

It may well be that Chretien was pressed into service to speak for special interests who found themselves in need of a mouthpiece. But if he did get into such a position, our next concern is how it happened, and that depends on the precise way the *Graal* meshed with current events.

Peculiar Circumstances

Conte del Graal was apparently written during the 1180's. Chretien had been spending most of his time in Troyes enjoying the hospitality of Henry and Marie of Champagne. But Henry died in 1181, shortly after returning from the Crusades. The next year, Philip of Flanders was calling on the widowed Marie, trying unsuccessfully to win her hand in marriage. And it was during this period that Chretien seems to have turned his professional attention to Philip.

Although these events imply a transition of some sort, that may not have been the case. Since the two courts were closely associated, Chretien's relationships with them might have been one continuous affair. We must remember that minstrels traveled freely from court to court, and Chretien may well have maintained close relationships with both courts at the same time. So while the story of the Grail was ostensibly written at the command of the Count of Flanders, Chretien could have drawn ideas from other members of the nobility as well.

Marie of Champagne, for example, was not just a pretty face. At a time when most women received little education and were expected to limit their activities to taking care of the house, she was actively involved in political and social issues and spent much of her time promoting an ideal code of conduct that served as the model for chivalry.

In any event, Philip returned from the Holy Land in 1179, and it was apparently during the following three or four years that the idea of turning the "book" into the *Graal* was born. But there is no reason to assume that this occurred in a vacuum.

Although French involvement in the Holy Land was ongoing – as shown by Philip and Henry's presence there – it was certainly not constant. The enthusiasm that accompanied the First Crusade at the beginning of the century had worn thin. The grim realities of waging hostilities in a foreign land took over, and many Europeans questioned the value of continuing the effort.

The last "official" effort had been the Second Crusade, and it ended in 1148 with a disastrous attack on Damascus. Interestingly, at least one Christian writer of the time put the failure of the Damascus siege down to treachery on the part of the Knights Templar. This may well be true. The political side of the Crusades was often less than honorable, and treachery among the Christians was only one sign of the complex situation in which they found themselves.

But nothing about the Crusades remained the same for long. By the end of the century, support for another Crusade was on the upswing. The passage of years had diminished the feeling of disillusionment among European leaders. And in 1165, in response to increasingly desperate calls for help from the Christian kingdom in Jerusalem, Pope Alexander III reissued an earlier crusading bull, *Quantum praedecessores*, and an income tax was levied the following year to support Christians in the Holy Land.

However, it still seemed unlikely that another Crusade was going to happen. One of the key reasons was the chronic bickering that existed between Henry II of England and Louis VII of France. They didn't trust each other, so neither was willing to go off to the Crusades and leave the other behind to cause trouble.

By the 1170s, it was obvious that peace between France and England had become a prerequisite of the Europeans' mounting a meaningful Third Crusade. But history has a way of making itself more complicated. Just when everything seemed perfectly predictable, Louis died and Philip of Flanders became regent of France. He ruled on behalf of the young heir to the throne, Philip Augustus, who in 1180 became king at the age of fifteen.

With all of this going on around him, Philip certainly had reasons for wanting to promote the values that soon appeared in written form in the *Graal*. A committed Crusader himself, he was keen on the idea of a Third Crusade. But there was resistance everywhere. Things were moving too slowly. And to make things worse, in the 1170's the Muslims got a new leader named Saladin, and he was beginning to pull the Infidels together as a unified force – something that rarely happened in that part of the world.

Not to put too fine a point on it, if the Christians of Europe didn't do something fast, it looked as if the Holy Land would be lost and the Crusades would be finished for good.

Clearly, people like Philip of Flanders and Marie of Champagne were the sort who got things done. They entertained lofty ideas. They had enough wealth and power to make others pay attention. They had the will to act. And they had one more thing that made it possible for them to be effective: they had what in today's parlance would be called a network.

Those associated with the noble courts of twelfth century Flanders and Champagne moved freely in channels that gave them access to others with similar values and interests. What they had could not be called an organization or a fraternity. It didn't have quite that level of formal structure. But it did in fact have some of the elements those words imply, not the least of which was both horizontal and vertical cohesion.

The nobility of that day certainly had what we would call horizontal cohesion. They were in close touch with their neighbors and felt strong bonds – bonds created partly by their fondness for political intrigue, to be sure – which gave them almost as much unity and an extended family might have.

But they also had vertical cohesion. They carried in their hearts the influence of strong traditions and a heritage which tied them to earlier generations. The nobles who lived at the end of the twelfth century – nobles like Philip, Henry and Marie – were bound by a common culture to those who lived at the beginning of the century – men like Hugh de Payens and Bernard of Clairvaux. And those bonds were as strong as the ones that bound them to their neighbors down the road.

Just as the stories told by the Breton minstrels held together over the years and improved with age, so did the people who moved within the network of the French nobility. They were able to draw from a cultural wellspring that gave them resources they could not have drawn from themselves as individuals.

In short, these people knew how to work together. And these were the people with whom Chretien de Troyes associated. He was in the middle of a hotbed of politics, and he certainly had connections with the nobility. But might he also have had connections with the Church?

Scholars are divided on whether Chretien was a priest. He knew how to read and write at a time when the Church was the sole custodian of literacy. Therefore he must at least have spent a fair amount of time with churchmen, and much of his writing has religious overtones. But whether he had a closer connection with the religious hierarchy – and therefore may have represented the Church's interests– is purely speculative.

Up to a certain point, all of this is perfectly normal. In those days many nobles went on crusade, some served as regents for young kings, minstrels traveled among royal courts and wrote poems for their patrons, and the Church was an ever present influence in those circles. But is there a pattern here, one that lies just below the surface?

In fact, a pattern does seem to be emerging. Philip of Flanders, a powerful and well connected nobleman, had just returned from the Holy Land and was interested in promoting another Crusade when he "commanded" the country's foremost – and presumably most capable – writer to prepare a work based on a "book." For some unknown reason, this book seems to have had a special meaning for the count. The writer acknowledged the importance of the book by calling it "the best story ever." Then he proceeded to write a very curious tale based on it. Just down the road was the place where the Knights Templar had received their marching orders. Their founder was born nearby, and the abbot who pushed the Order's charter through the Church bureaucracy had also worked in the neighborhood.

And lest we think Philip's sojourn in the Holy Land was a passing fancy or an experience he wanted to put behind him, it is worth noting that he went on crusade again in 1190 and died in the Holy Land the following year. Thus his commitment to the Crusades – or at least to something that was going on in the Holy Land – really was a serious and ongoing matter.

Philip's commission to write the *Graal* occurred in the midst of all this and may well have been connected to it. But the web of relationships that binds these characters in place and time is not enough to prove that. To draw a connection between Chretien's last poem and the Templars we must extract more evidence from an era in which evidence is hard to find. And the evidence is in the poem itself.

Old Sources and New Ideas

Over the years, much has been made of similarities between the Grail story and initiation rites, both ancient and modern. There is no doubt that these similarities exist and in some cases are quite striking. But the fact that such works as Chretien's *Graal* correspond in detail with the ancient mystery religions and with the initiation rituals of modern fraternities must be handled with care.

All teachers learn early in their careers that when two students give the same correct answer to an exam question, the conclusion that one copied from the other is unwarranted. The students may have studied together. They may have studied the same material independently of each other. Or acquired the same knowledge from different sources. Or approached the test in complete ignorance and merely benefited from the same amount of luck.

The fact that organizations with initiation ceremonies have a way of "getting it right" also falls short of proving they copied from each other. They may have. But they may have drawn from the same sources, either in concert or independently. Or they may simply have drawn from the same well of wisdom.

All initiations are a way of getting from one place to another, so they always have a symbolic journey, even if it isn't explicitly described as such. And all initiates hope to get something for their initiation fee, so the initiation needs to involve a quest of some sort and the eventual reward of gaining something new.

More to the point, since ancient legends have been published since ancient times, organizations have always had access to the same building blocks. So it should come as no surprise that their ceremonies display a remarkable sameness.

In other words, when everything looks alike, looking alike no longer matters.

Having said all of this, and knowing that Chretien drew from old sources, we must still deal with one more interesting fact. Both the knight on a quest and the grail as a sacred object seem to find their origin in the pen of Chretien de Troyes.

At this point it is worth recalling that in the twelfth century writers worked on commission. Their patrons told them what to write, and they used their skills to do the job properly – i.e., with the flair and imagination the patron generally lacked.

The conclusion of this point is obvious. The words were Chretien's but the idea of the questing knight and the Holy Grail almost certainly came from Philip of Flanders, with the possible assistance of others who were working behind the scenes. Book or no book, it was not the writer but the politician who created these concepts.

When we look at Chretien's poem with this in mind, we notice two curious things. The story of the Grail is loaded with symbols, and those symbols coincide precisely with the quest for sacred relics on which the Templars had supposedly embarked.

Of course, symbolism was not rare among twelfth century Europeans; they were all afflicted by it. But symbolism always serves a purpose, and the purpose it serves in Chretien's *Graal* lies at the heart of our inquiry.

Scholars have traced large sections of the Arthurian romances to ancient Welsh and Irish legends. And the Arthurian versions of these stories clearly retain pagan elements from the original sources. But as time went on those elements were restated and redefined to carry Christian messages.

The symbols that appear in the *Graal*, in particular, provide a good example of this. Several of the poem's episodes bear striking similarities to older stories. Many bits and pieces, both large and small, seem to have been lifted intact from Welsh and Irish sources, and it is reasonable to assume that Chretien knew very well where the material came from. But he gives his version a decidedly Christian cast.

More than that, his poem often has the feel of something written by a journalist. It could easily be a fictional account of current events, not unlike modern novels that are based on recent history.

This point is reinforced by the novelty of the poem's contents. Since both the questing knight and the Templar were new on the European stage, stories about them would have to contain new material – or at least new ideas – mixed in with anything drawn from older sources.

Perceval and the Templars

In particular, Chretien writes about the young Perceval, a knight who embarked on a quest to rediscover the Grail when he learned it had supernatural powers. He needed to find the Grail because he once had it in sight but let it slip away when he failed to recognize its true value.

This is not the story of the old Irish and Welsh legends. It is a new twist on old themes, a "modern" invention that arose at the time of the Crusades. And it is closely related to the early history of the Knights Templar.

The Crusades began at the very end of the eleventh century, and with them was born the idea of the warrior who journeyed to the Holy Land to wrest what was sacred from the hands of the Infidel. The Templars were an early product of that development, and with them was born the idea of an organization that was both standing army and religious Order. Thus the military venture and the quest for the sacred combined to form a single notion, and its highest expression was the Templar.

We have seen that the Templars began the process of redefining themselves shortly after the council of Troyes. But how far they went in changing their mandate is a question that has never been fully answered. Even in their own day, they were suspected of a wide range of extra curricular activities ranging from the sacred to the diabolical.

This picture is complicated by the prosecution of the Order for heresy some two centuries after they were founded. The trials and execution of more than a few Templars lent credence to the rumors, although much of the evidence against them was clearly false. Still, there is evidence that the Templars did things their original mandate didn't call for them to do.

To be precise, there is reason to believe that, once they were in the Holy Land, the Templars took it upon themselves to rediscover such sacred relics as the Ark of the Covenant, the cup from the Last Supper and Jesus' burial shroud. In fact, it is just possible that Hugh de Payens and his comrades actually organized the Templars to continue a quest for sacred relics they had already started. Even in their early years, it appears that the Templars went to considerable trouble searching for religious artifacts, when their mandate only called for them to protect pilgrims and fight the Infidel.

It is basically the same story Chretien told in *Conte del Graal*. Perceval, like the Templars, departs from the normal duties of a knight, learns that sacred relics and spiritual insight are available, then embarks on a long and difficult quest to obtain them.

This may be a coincidence, but it provides an enticing hint that the Grail story in its original form does tie in with actual events of the day. And it is reinforced by another clue.

After leaving the Grail castle, Perceval encounters a character known as the Weeping Maiden. This incident and the question and answer session which follows have always been regarded as peculiar. But to the informed observer they have the unmistakable ring of the catechisms so common in Freemasonry.

As Perceval recounts his experience in the Grail castle, he is greeted with a series of questions summarizing his recent experience and highlighting its important points. Moreover, this is done in a form that could easily be used for ritual purposes. The passage reads in part:

"And did you see the grail?
"Quite clearly.
"Who carried it?
"A maiden.
"Where did she come from?
"From a chamber.
"And where did she go?
"She entered another chamber.
"Did anyone precede the grail?
"Yes.
"Who?
"Only two squires.
"And what were they holding in their hands?
"Candelabra full of candles.
"And who came after the grail?
"Another maiden.
"What was she holding?
"A small silver carving platter."

This is a curious bit of verse. For a start, it doesn't reveal anything new to the reader. In addition, it gives the Weeping Maiden knowledge she presumably would not have had. And, finally, it does not seem to serve any purpose. Even in the tradition of oral story telling, where things are often repeated to remind the listener of important points and to keep a narrative from becoming confusing because of its length and complexity, Perceval's exchange with the Weeping Maiden seems unnecessary.

It may, however, be far from unnecessary. In fact, it may be one of the most essential parts of the poem. For there is an interpretation of this passage – and of the context in which we find it – that pulls together all of the baffling and seemingly unrelated pieces of the puzzle.

If the *Graal* really does dovetail with the contemporary history of the Templars, it is just possible that they coincide in more than content. The poem may actually have been meant to function as a veiled account of the Templars' enterprise. But if so, it was not their avowed enterprise of protecting pilgrims and fighting the Infidel. It was the more clandestine – and never officially acknowledged – business of scouring the Holy Land for Christianity's most sacred relics.

Then are we looking at a document which served a ritual purpose? Was it indeed written for or about the Templars, and if so, what was it supposed to accomplish?

An Initiation Ritual?

Clearly Chretien has not given us a full blown ritual in the modern sense, either military or Masonic or even fraternal in the most general terms. However, a close examination of his text reveals that it contains the same elements that make up the essence of today's Masonic ritual. More important, these elements are in the correct order, and taken as a group they reflect a perspective that has often been called the "spirit of Masonry." An overview of *Conte del Graal* shows how striking the parallels are.

Early in the poem, while Chretien is still setting the tone and mapping out the subject matter of his story, he has Perceval encounter a group of knights. The youth has never seen knights before and quickly decides that he wants to be one of them. In other words, he wants to join their organization.

The next few lines consist of a question and answer session in which the knights give brief explanations of the uses to which they put their weapons and armor. This obviously parallels Masonic descriptions of the Craft's working tools. But it is by no means an initiation. It is a superficial description of the sort an inquisitive non-mason might hear when he asks a Mason about the Fraternity.

This dialog is enough, however, to make Perceval take the next step. His determination to become a knight is strengthened, and he asks where he can find King Arthur, who has the authority to make him a knight. Here, too, Perceval follows the course of the modern initiate. He has taken the first step by asking about the organization and, believing it has something to offer him, he has taken the second step by seeking initiation.

Although this episode may seem incidental, it is in fact the starting point for everything that follows. One characteristic of any organization which employs moral instruction is that its members – not to mention prospective members – must "seek" before they can "find." The basic nature of moral insight, as opposed to ordinary knowledge, is that it requires both a desire to learn and an ability to understand. Therefore, Perceval and all other initiates, either ancient or modern, must "desire and inquire" before they can step up and receive their instruction.

Perceval follows this pattern, and when he finally locates Arthur his request for initiation is granted, but a curious twist occurs. When the king tells Perceval to dismount and kneel to be knighted in proper form, the young man refuses. He insists on being knighted while still mounted.

We are inclined to believe that this *faux pas* arises from the youth's ignorance. But could there be another explanation?

Perceval has just been knighted, but in a very real sense he is not yet a knight. The ceremony is incomplete, leaving more to be done. This has the effect, which we believe is one of Chretien's most deliberate allusions, of anticipating a more complex initiation. The issue is presented in mediaeval terms but is something the modern ritualist will recognize immediately.

When a Masonic candidate receives the first degree, he becomes a Mason, but this does not mean that he is really a Mason. His status is ambiguous precisely because of the progressive nature of the ritual. The candidate has taken only the first step, which is incomplete, and it remains for him to pursue his initiation further in other degrees. Only then will he fully inherit the mantle of the craft he has entered.

The fact that the modern ritual requires more than one degree is no accident. When the medieval craft evolved into a social and philosophical organization in the 18th century, it developed a body of symbolism so elaborate and multi-layered that it could not be accommodated by the single ceremony of the operative masons. It required two, and eventually three ceremonies, each of which built on material presented in the previous session and added a richer layer of meaning to it.

In the *Graal*, we see an early version of this. Chretien seems to be telling us that while Perceval has become a knight, he has not completed the process. He has more to do before he personifies all that is contained in the ideal of knighthood.

At this point, Perceval becomes a "traveling man." Although that term is popular in Masonic circles, it apparently wasn't used in Chretien's time. Yet the sense of it comes through very clearly in the journeys on which the young Perceval now embarks. He visits a series of castles, which seem to symbolize the various levels of his initiation. They are three in number, consistent with the Christian symbolism of the Trinity. But the number is also dictated by the logical structure of the lessons the young man encounters.

At the first level, he receives more information about the knight's "working tools." Perceval is taught how to use his weapons and armor. And he is given basic training in such matters as how to treat a lady and when to grant mercy to a defeated opponent.

This episode includes Perceval's introductory lesson in the obligations of a knight. He is, for example, told that he must grant mercy when asked to do so, and he must avoid talking too much. Like its modern Masonic equivalent, this initial discourse on duty is not explained. Perceval is asked to commit himself to an obligation, but he clearly does not understand the "why" of the duties which have been imposed on him.

Perceval then proceeds to another castle, where he learns more. He begins to understand the moral implications of his knightly duties when he sees at first hand the devastating effect of siege warfare. He tries to help, but his efforts only complicate the situation. In trying to defend the castle and, as a result, dealing with a defeated opponent, he proposes a series of penalties. However, when the opponent complains that they will unfairly cost him his life, Perceval enters into a bit of give and take, forcing him to confront the consequences of his actions.

Like his modern Masonic counterpart, Perceval has moved from the mechanics of his craft to its moral dimension. The use of his "working tools," which he learned earlier, has propelled him to a higher level of understanding.

Perceval then visits a third castle, where he encounters the Fisher King, the Grail and the bleeding lance. He has thus progressed from the mechanical and moral to the spiritual. He is shown symbols with profound meaning, but their significance is withheld from him. That he must find for himself.

In this way the young knight encounters yet another aspect of initiation. Just when he must have thought he had learned everything, he discovers that there is much more to his quest than he imagined.

Like the modern initiate, he voluntarily and cheerfully entered the ranks of a fraternity but had little knowledge of what he was getting into. Once inside, he accepted obligations he did not understand. He encountered moral truths he may not have expected. He found a spiritual dimension beyond anything for which his earlier experience had prepared him. And now he finds that he has only just begun. Now he learns that he must pursue the rest of the quest by himself, building on the lessons he has received in an effort to discover the meanings of symbols whose importance he did not, and perhaps could not previously grasp.

This marks the conclusion of Perceval's formal initiation, and it is time for him to take the lessons he has learned into the real world, where he will seek the moral and spiritual benefits he now knows are available. Having experienced the three levels of his initiation, he has not failed to appreciate their relevance to his own life. And that, of course, was the point of it all.

The remaining verses of the *Graal* deal with the life long applications of the wisdom Perceval acquired during his initiation, but we need not dwell on this material. While it is an important part of the story, our investigation centers on the web of connections that link the Grail with the lodge, and it is Perceval's desire to be a knight plus his initiation which show us those connections.

A Real Initiation Ritual?

When we follow the youth through his adventures, we feel that the poem's symbolism points to something other than fantasy. Just below the surface it has a tangible quality which seems to imply more than a writer's imagination.

In addition, obvious parallels with the modern ritual point to things that go beyond fiction. Chretien has indeed presented us with the essential elements of a fraternal initiation. Those elements survive relatively intact in the Masonic ritual as it developed in the 18th century. But if they were attached to a real ceremony in the 18th century, could they have been part of something equally as real in the 12th?

In other words, was there something quite substantial to which the "Percevals" of Chretien's day were attracted? And did it offer an unexpected spiritual quest to naive youths who at first sought only the glamour and adventure they saw on the surface?

If the *Graal* does reflect a real life quest that was unfolding as part of the Crusades, we still need to understand its message and function. Again, we turn to the poem itself.

Perceval is represented as naive and uneducated, even by medieval standards. This is the key to his character, and it is exploited early in the story. While staying at the castle of one Gornemant de Gorhaut, Perceval is warned not to ask too many questions.

What we see unfolding here is a carefully constructed picture of a young, medieval knight. Perceval is a product of the rigid society of his day, and his character is a reflection of his environment. People of all classes were expected to accept their positions and not challenge either their feudal superiors or the Church. To keep everyone in line, they received no more education than they needed to occupy their proper place in society, and they were discouraged from exploring things they didn't need to know.

While the knight occupied a privileged position in this system, he was bound by the same rules as everyone else. He didn't need a formal education to do his job. As a result, most knights were illiterate; they were trained in the skills of the warrior but little else. So it appears that Perceval's brief training in the castle represents what little education a knight of his day would have received.

As he puts his training behind him, the youth continues his journey and soon comes to the Grail castle, where he is entertained as a guest of the Fisher King, who owns the castle. There he encounters two curious items:

the Grail and a bleeding lance. At first he doesn't understand their meaning, but he later realizes they are sacred objects.

These objects are apparently holy not in their own right but because of their function. The Grail is holy because of what it holds, and the lance is for some reason that isn't specified in this version of the legend. (In later versions it is revealed as the lance which pierced Christ's side.)

In other words, these objects are presented in the story as things that have a symbolic quality. They stand for something else, something that is yet to be understood.

After Perceval leaves the Grail castle, he learns that if he had asked the right questions about these objects, a series of redemptive events would have occurred. Although he was inclined to ask, he bowed to the instruction he had previously received and held his tongue.

The young knight also learns the significance of the miraculous objects he saw, but they are now beyond his reach. He cannot retrace his steps and simply ask the questions he should have asked. (He later learns that he could not ask the proper questions because of a sin he had committed earlier.)

Perceval swears that he will undertake a quest to locate the Grail and lance and avail himself of their redemptive powers. He will not rest (i.e., spend two nights in the same lodging) or shrink from fighting any knight who opposes him until he succeeds. The quest proves long and difficult, but Perceval is sustained when his spirits flag by learning that he, too, is a descendant of the Fisher King's father, a strange character who was present – but never seen – at the Grail castle.

At this point, Chretien promises to return to Perceval and reveal the end of the story, but he never does. Most scholars have followed the lead of the *Graal*'s first editor, Gerbert de Montreuil, who stated barely a generation later that the poet died before finishing his work. But perhaps there is another explanation. It may be that the story did not have an ending during

Chretien's lifetime because it really was about the Templars, and the Templars had not yet found the sacred relics for which they were searching.

The scenario is simple. A large body of religious lore had existed in the Holy Land for many centuries. When Christian pilgrims began frequenting those climes, they were exposed to this lore and found it entertaining to say the least. They repeated and embellished many of the stories they heard. Over time, the stories became even more fabulous than they were when the Christians first heard them, and many of them had to do with the whereabouts of sacred relics from the time of Jesus and his disciples.

When the Templars arrived in the eleventh century, they heard the current versions of these stories. The Templars found them impressive, because they were hearing many of them for the first time. Until the Crusades began, the Holy Land was a faraway place, and European Christians knew little of what occurred there. Now the Templars were hearing about sacred relics, and suddenly new horizons seemed to open before them. The platter that served bread at the Last Supper, the cup Jesus offered to his disciples, the shroud that covered his body, all of these might still exist somewhere. And if they could be found, they might reward their finders by giving up some of their marvelous redemptive powers.

But finding these relics would not be easy. In a hostile land, riddled with strife and Infidels, the quest for long lost relics would take courage and perseverance. The Templars would have to deal with the Infidel. They would have to ask questions (perhaps forbidden questions, considering the closed society of the day), seek in sordid places, and neither rest nor shrink from fighting any enemy who opposed them. They were, after all, spiritual sons of God, just as Perceval was the spiritual son of the Fisher King's father. If they were steadfast and faithful and purged themselves of the sins like the one that had kept Perceval from asking questions in the Grail castle, they would be entitled to the reward waiting at the end of their quest.

This is the message the Templars needed to instill in the minds of their recruits if they wanted to search for sacred relics. And that may well be the reason Philip commissioned Chretien to write the first Grail story. While it might inspire the people of Europe to support the Crusades, it would certainly provide a fine indoctrination for Templar initiates.

If this was the purpose of the *Graal*, it may have been intended partly as a public relations tool to create support on the home front. The evidence suggests that it was well received when it was eventually released to the public. But the work's curious, almost ritualistic tone, along with its peculiar use of symbolism to promote the Templars' enterprise, suggest another use. We can imagine that the story was read to Templar recruits during their long journey to the Holy Land. It would be a convenient way to teach young, uneducated knights the moral values for which they would soon be fighting.

Perhaps the Order even used the poem – or sections of it – in an initiation ritual to portray a dramatic scene, just as the Freemasons use dramatic scenes in their initiations today. It is clearly the story of a quest, and it clearly conveys the values the Templars would have wished their recruits to have.

The men who joined the Order came from the rigid society of medieval Europe. They were raised to accept authority and not ask too many questions. But when they enlisted in the Order of the Temple and journeyed to the Holy Land, they had to have a new set of loyalties and sensibilities. And if they were expected to enter into a clandestine search for holy relics as well, they would certainly need a commitment to ideals that were unheard of in Europe.

The Need for Secrecy

It may be that the concepts of the questing knight and the Grail were produced not by the Crusades themselves but by a crusade within a crusade, a quest that required a new set of teaching tools. But why couch all of this in symbolism?

The most obvious reason is that the medieval Frenchman thought in symbols. Consequently, symbols were the easiest and most direct way to impart information to him. Many knights were illiterate, and getting them to think in pictorial form was a natural teaching method. (The Tarot cards, which appeared mysteriously in western Europe at the same time as the Grail legends, are thought to have had a similar purpose, although the precise message they were trying to get across is now lost.)

On a more practical level, the most important rule of treasure hunting is to say as little as possible. Even in a land crawling with Infidels, the threat of competition undoubtedly worried the Templars and contributed to their notorious cult of secrecy.

And a third reason was the public relations problem the Templars had to deal with. As they continued their work in the Holy Land, the taint of heresy began to surround them.

By the time Chretien was commissioned to write his poem, the Order may well have encountered such "errors" as the Gnostic Gospels. They undoubtedly came face to face with the Moslem religion and a variety of eastern cults. Until the Crusades began, these beliefs were little more than rumors in western Europe. Now the Templars were in direct contact with them, and they must have realized from the start how dangerous dealing with such heresies was going to be.

If, as many scholars claim, the Templars actually dabbled in these matters, they would certainly have known how precarious their position was. Looking outside the iron-bound confines of Church theology was a dangerous practice and one best clouded in symbolism and secrecy.

With such reasons as these to be less than candid, the Templars could certainly appreciate the benefits of taking an indirect approach. If the *Graal* was a document intended least partly for internal consumption, it could easily have functioned this way. It could be used as an indoctrination lecture for recruits or an advanced ritual for the inner circle who were privy to the Order's real secrets. For this purpose, it contained all the symbolism needed to enlighten the initiated, while expressing everything in such vague terms that it was sure to confound the outsider.

Perhaps this was their plan from the beginning. The poem may not at first have been intended for others to see. We must remember that *Conte del Graal* was apparently not released to the public until after both Philip and Chretien were dead, and then perhaps without the knowledge or permission of any surviving individuals who had an interest in it.

In any event, it is too late to reconstruct the precise nature of the ritual this poem may once have been. By the time its verses reached us, they had undergone heavy editing. Many scholars believe the sections dealing with Perceval and Gawain were in fact two unfinished works that were spliced together after Chretien's death. Separating them is easy. But once we have isolated the Perceval portion, it is impossible to tell how much it was altered since it left Chretien's hand. Copyists and editors of the day did not hesitate to embellish the works entrusted to them, and even the earliest copies of the *Graal* may contain a great deal of added material.

Nevertheless, we have good reason to believe that somewhere in the lines of this poem, with its unique portrayal of the questing knight and the Grail, lie words heard by Templar initiates in secret chambers as they embarked on the most wonderful journey they could imagine. But if Chretien's poem was designed to serve as a ritual for the Templars, or at least to reflect the Templar ritual and credo, how does it connect with the modern Masonic ritual?

The First Masonic Ritual

Obviously the poem contains an enduring collection of moral precepts from which more than one modern organization has borrowed. The Freemasons, in particular, have made much of the elements of this "first" Grail story.

109

Perceval is described as "the son of the widow lady." He embarks on a quest for important moral truth, and the goal of that quest is a reward that comes at the end of a well spent life. All of these are themes that loom large in Masonic symbolism.

The castle in which Perceval dines is even reminiscent of a setting employed by the Royal Order of Scotland. But castles are common enough, and a castle is as good a setting for an ancient degree as any other location.

Still, there may be a slender thread leading from the *Graal* to the lodge. We have seen that the modern ritual inherited elements of medieval Scottish masonry, which in turn recalled historic connections between the Templars and the Scots during Scotland's struggle for independence. We have also seen that the workings of the Royal Order of Scotland contain a survival of an early Masonic ritual, which preserved the legend that the Royal Order was founded by Robert Bruce to reward fugitive Templars who came to his aid at Bannockburn.

Here we may, at long last, have a fleeting glimpse of the medieval Templars' input into that ancient Masonic working. It came from a document the Order originally used to promote its quest for sacred relics. When the Order was suppressed a little more than a century later, a few of its members carried the document, or at least the ideas it contained, to Scotland. There the fugitive knights joined in the struggle for Scottish independence, and when they were rewarded with a new, secret Order of knighthood, they drew from their old initiation rites to make a ritual for their new Order.

Their old rites were, after all, the only ritual these knights knew outside the Church litany. It was only natural for them to use it when they recreated their old Order in a new form. So elements from the first Grail story became the foundation for a new ritual.

In short, we believe that a Templar "working" is reflected in Chretien's re-working of the material he received from Count Philip of Flanders. And that material comes to us, through a glass very darkly indeed, in the ritual of modern Freemasonry.

The religious symbolism in this ritual made it into an enduring set of lessons that has stood up well during the centuries since it was first committed to paper. It is no wonder that it survived. But one question about the origin of this marvelous story remains. We still have to take another look at Chretien's statement about his source.

Although it seems that Chretien deliberately concealed much of what he was up to, one of his statements now has an unmistakable ring of truth. He said that his story of the Grail was based on a book that contained the best ever told in a royal court. Those words – "the best story ever told" - have a curious and familiar tone. Could it be a deliberate, though veiled, reference to what Chretien and his fellows would have considered truly the best story ever told: the central theme of the Gospels? And could the book from which Chretien drew the story, the book he received from his patron with a command that he commit a story from it to verse, have been a copy of the New Testament?

Temple Old Church, Midlothian, Scotland
Situated within a few miles of both Rosslyn and Seton, this building served as headquarters for Templar activities in southern Scotland

Chretien's poem obviously forms a bridge between the pagan mythology of the old Celtic stories and the Christian symbolism of the later Grail legends. But more than that, it served as a point of departure for a new tradition that made something quite different out of the old traditions. During the century that followed the publication of the *Graal*, the notions of the questing knight and the search for religious relics crystallized into the essence of a Christian parable. Stories of King Arthur and the Round Table spread and gained popularity until they became the rage of Europe. And from that time on they never lost their appeal.

Monks from the Cistercian Order, which was closely associated with the rise of the Templars, were apparently the driving force behind many of the later Grail stories. Understandably, they introduced their Order's central tenets - charity, chastity and grace – into what had once been a pagan legend. The Grail became a vessel holding Christ's blood, and the lance (whose function was not identified in Chretien's version) became the weapon that pierced Christ's side on the cross.

As entire cycles of Grail stories appeared, they picked up this thread, drawing more and more on stories from the Gospels for their inspiration, but always with a haunting air of nostalgia. They all tell of something pure and valuable that was lost. And they consistently portray the Templars as the proper and rightful custodians of the thing that was lost.

Certainly that's the way Robert Bruce's Templars would have seen it. They felt they had been unjustly stripped of their honor and their role as champions of the faith … and as the proper custodians of the Grail. As their new organization evolved over the centuries, they cultivated their old ideals along with new legends, some of which were penned by writers who weren't aware the Templars had actually survived.

In time, even the descendants of those last Templars forgot their origins. As their organization continued to evolve, it retained its ritual's symbolism but forgot much of the meaning. It was only the Scottish Masons who kept the legend alive, and they did so only because they were determined to leave clues to where they had come from.

In a strange way, the story has come full circle. The Royal Order's veiled account of the Templars' last battle was not new. It preserved fragments of a story that goes all the way back to the twelfth century – to the very origins of what became the Masonic Fraternity. It was, indeed, the first Freemasons who created *that* story.

On the other hand, in a very real sense it was the story that created the Fraternity. It was Chretien's original work which actually shaped the role the Templars would play in history by eloquently defining for them the enterprise on which they were about to embark. He drew from the Gospels to give them a declaration of their goals and aspirations. Without his contribution, they would have remained just one of the many groups of Crusading knights who fought in the Holy Land. It was his declaration that shaped their quest and eventually served them as a ritual.

If this is the true version of the story behind the story, in the closing years of the twelfth century Chretien de Troyes engaged in his own quest. It was a quest very similar to the one embraced by the Freemasons of six centuries later. And by working on behalf of the Templars and their friends, he provided the inspiration for, if not the ancestor of, the modern Masonic degrees.

Anyone who wants to read the earliest Masonic ritual need only go to the nearest public library. The Craft's oldest ritual is carefully hidden, as are all Masonic truths. But it can be found in the lines of Chretien's last and best remembered poem.

Carving, Seton Old Church, Midlothian, Scotland

Thought by some to have Masonic significance, the carving may represent the murdered apprentice, mirroring carvings in Rosslyn Chapel.

CHAPTER 5

FROM TEMPLAR TO MASON

Old Wisdom Made New Again

WHEN Chretien used the Gospels to fashion the world's first Grail story, he brought their central theme to life in a unique and extraordinary way. He certainly could not have realized what he was accomplishing. He had fallen into one of those happy accidents of history that has a way of changing everything, but neither he nor any of the other players in the drama could have seen where their actions would lead.

It isn't that Chretien and his friends failed to appreciate what they were doing. They understood very well the nature of the Grail story they were creating. After all, they lived in a world dominated by the Bible and its lessons. To them, religion and religious symbolism were an important part of everyone's life. So it was perfectly natural for the French nobles of the day to adapt stories from the Gospels to produce a poem that would help the Templars in their quest for sacred relics in the Holy Land. But what they did not – and perhaps could not – appreciate was the elegance with which their poem captures the essence of the sacred quest.

In a few lines they told the story of one person's search for truth, wisdom and insight in his own life. The search symbolized the Templars' journey through two centuries of their official existence. Later, it gave them a model for the course they pursued after their Order had supposedly died and ceased to exist. And still later it became the foundation for a timeless allegory that goes to the heart of the Gospel message.

116

The central theme of the Gospels can be summed up by the familiar words "seek and ye shall find." In the context of the scriptures, those words embody the human race's universal longing for spiritual insight and salvation. But in Chretiens' *Conte del Graal* they become a blueprint for a well spent life.

In the closing years of the twelfth century, Chretien and the Templars turned the Gospels' theme into the story of a quest. And in doing so they gave the world the beginning of a marvelous adventure.

Perhaps without realizing it, they had devised a multi-layered story that symbolizes each person's journey. It deals with a universal need to understand the purpose and meaning of life. And it presents itself in the form of a glamorous tale of knights in shining armor, fair damsels, exotic settings and the kind of adventure most people can never hope to experience for themselves.

Few can resist being drawn into such a story, and once there, everyone can have the vicarious experience of engaging in the quest. In the end, that was Chretien's contribution. No longer were these ideas the domain of priests and theologians. They had suddenly become – and would forever remain – a fantasy even the simplest mind could grasp.

When *Conte del Graal* was published a few years after Chretien's death, the story became the property of the world. It caught on almost immediately, and since then the quest for the Grail has taken its place among the most popular themes of literature.

Chretien and the Templars told the story in a form which may, even in their day, have been used as a ritual. But since their time, it has played a complex role and has taken many guises. It became a foundation for much of the Arthurian cycle. It has become commonplace in literature and language, providing the basic plots for any number of books, plays and movies, and lending many figures of speech to the language.

But of all the versions of the story that survive to this day, the Masonic version is in many ways the most faithful to the original. It contains a body of symbols that can not be mistaken for anything other than symbols. And those symbols remain close to their original intent. By their own admission they point the way to the reward for a well spent life, and that was the whole point of Chretien's story.

Of course, nothing remains the same. The "masons" of Bannockburn were the direct heirs of the remarkable web of people and events who created the original concept of the quest. Those masons must certainly have received the story in its purest and most unadulterated form. As Chretien's story traveled through the centuries, however, it experienced any number of changes. And recognizing the Masonic version as a descendant of Chretien's *Graal* is not easy.

When the Templars brought their ritual to Scotland, they did so as warrior monks. The ritual and legends they preserved in their new Order of knighthood – the one that evolved into the Royal Order of Scotland – may well have been presented in the same words Chretien wrote for them slightly more than a century earlier. But when it emerged from the Middle Ages three centuries later, it was clothed in the symbolism of the stone masons' lodge.

We have seen how this occurred historically, but why it occurred in not immediately obvious. So it may be worth a few additional comments.

Although the change may appear drastic and arbitrary, the connection between the Templars and the masons is not as remote as it might seem. As a military Order, the Templars used stone fortifications extensively. In fact, they were famous in their own time for having the best fortresses in the world. They certainly dealt with stone masons on a routine basis, and architecture was one of the professions the Templars nurtured among their ranks.

In the Middle Ages, both the Templar and the stone mason were closely connected with the Church. The Templars evolved as a monastic Order, and the masons were trained professionals at a time when all education was in the hands of churchmen. In fact, the men who operated the masons' lodges of that era were not common laborers but skilled architects and craftsmen. Most were monks, and all had close ties with monastic Orders.

It is not surprising, then, that the Templars and the masons knew each other. And when the Templars found themselves stripped of their original mission, it is likely that many of them drifted into the stone masons' profession. If so, the details of the transformation have been lost. That isn't surprising, either. We wouldn't expect the fugitive knights of the fourteenth century to leave a record of their activities, so the evolution from warrior to stone worker has left only a tenuous thread in the fabric of Masonic history.

It is not hard to understand the situation the Templars faced in the years following the battle of Bannockburn. They were local heroes, but they were also fugitives. At the end of their trials in France, the Church had ordered them to disband. It was an order that carried with it the full force of law, and violating it could have brought individual Templars death as relapsed heretics.

But they were unwilling to let their Order simply die. So they kept it going in a new guise, as the Order their friend Robert Bruce had created for them. But where would they go and what would they do?

When they became fugitives, it is reasonable to assume that they did in fact associate themselves with masons with whom they had enjoyed close relations for years. Thus the Templar wisdom that started with Chretien merged with the sculptures of the stone mason and the rich symbolism of the gothic cathedral.

The way Chretien's story was handed from the Templars to the masons is shrouded in the mists of the Scottish lowlands. But there is little doubt that the stone masons did inherit it. It can't be mere coincidence that during the century after Bannockburn the Sinclair family built the world famous Rosslyn Chapel not far from the battlefield. The Sinclairs supported a large number of artisans who appeared seemingly from nowhere to build the chapel. It was even necessary to found a village nearby to house them.

119

The result of their effort was an incredible array of stone carvings which contain unmistakable bits of Templar and Masonic imagery. Nor can it be pure coincidence that the Seton family built their own chapel, Seton Old Church, at the same time, and that the architecture of their chapel, too, shows signs of a Templar legacy.

In the ornately carved walls of those chapels, and in the streets of Rosslyn village, we see evidence of a new form of the masons' lodge. It now had a dual heritage: the stone masons who traced their origins to the building of King Solomon's Temple and the knights who traced theirs to the field of Bannockburn and before that to the Crusades.

For centuries the new lodges preserved their dual heritage in the *Old Constitutions*, the original of which was written within a generation of Bannockburn. At this document's heart lies the York Legend, a veiled account of the Templars' dealings with Robert Bruce but curiously set in a northern county of England once largely owned by the Templars.

When they wrote the *Old Constitutions* the Masons started the process of building their legend. They were already combining the old Temlpar ritual with the stone masons' lore, and their curious blend of ideas was tempered with the story of how a group of fugitive knights received a new Order. This was the material that would gradually evolve into the modern Masonic ritual.

Of course, the story at the core of the ritual changed over the years. As it traveled from twelfth century France to Scotland and then to England, the young questing knight, Perceval, was transformed into a stone mason and then into the poor initiate who is portrayed in today's lodge ceremonies.

For practical reasons, the involvement of the fugitive Templars in Masonic affairs was at first kept secret. But as time passed, both the Templars and their enemies became relics of history. Their story receded into legend, and any real need for secrecy disappeared.

Seton Church, Midlothian, Scotland

Built by the Setons, a Norman-Flemish family with close links to the Templars, this church features Templar gravestones and obvious examples of Masonic imagery.

Rosslyn Chapel, Midlothian, Scotland

Like those in Seton Church, the elaborate carvings in Rosslyn Chapel are rich in Templar and Masonic Imagery. Seen here is the famous Apprentice's Pillar, which reputedly symbol-

Eventually, the details were of interest only to the families whose ancestors were actually involved in the events and to the Masons whose legends now included bits of the story. It was those Scottish families and Scottish Masons who preserved the story, while the rest of the world moved on.

When James I and his court moved to London, they certainly took their Scottish brand of Masonry with them. By this time the craft was already starting its evolution into a fraternal organization. Some of the lodges that would soon band together to form modern Freemasonry were still operative, composed mainly of stone masons. But they were already at the beginning of a major period of transition. With the world changing around them, they had to look to the future. That meant the lodges had to adapt, and their ritual had to adapt, too.

By the time the eighteenth century arrived, the Masons were well on their way to becoming a modern organization, and that marked the end of an era. When many of the ritual's medieval elements fell away during the transition, the last traces of the heritage of Bannockburn slipped away as well. Bits of the symbolism that had told its story were still there. But they were now obscure icons that no one understood any more.

Students of the Craft's ritual can confirm that the ceremonies have several quaint symbols which seem out of place. Their meanings are unknown; even experts in the field can only guess at them. They must have meant something originally, but the reason they were once considered important enough to add to the ritual has been lost, and now they are only curious relics no one appreciates.

The Craft's Scottish heritage was headed for the same fate. Perhaps it was a victim of its own history. It had been kept too secret, even for the Masons. And in the early years of the eighteenth century, it was in danger of being forgotten altogether.

That's when the Scottish Masons were spurred into action. Seeing the last remnants of their cherished heritage slipping away, a group of them struggled to preserve the story of their ancestors' role in creating the Fraternity. It was, after all, their story, and in their minds it deserved a place in the ritual.

A close examination of the Grand Lodge's struggles during those days shows a determined effort by the Scots to influence the way the Fraternity saw its past. The record indicates that the central issue was the Fraternity's traditions. It came down to whether the lodges were going to hold to their "Old Institutions" or turn away from them.

There is compelling evidence that James Anderson approached the Grand Lodge early in its existence and suggested to its leaders that they needed a revised copy of the *Old Constitutions* as a document to define their new organization. A little more than a decade later, another Scot, Michael Andrew Ramsay, introduced – or reintroduced – the notion that the Masons traced their heritage to the Crusading knights. Within another decade or so, a new Masonic organization was formed, claiming that it intended to reinstate the older, more traditional form of the ritual. And its ritual claimed that Masonry arose from the bloody field of Bannockburn.

During this entire period, a schism was brewing. It was about issues which seem trivial, unless there was more to them than appears on the surface. But we can now see that at bottom the dispute was about the old traditions – the features of Freemasonry which defined what the organization had been.

This brings the Scottish initiative full circle. The *Old Constitutions* was based on a work that was written within a generation of Bannockburn. It includes the story of a change in the Masonic organization, a veiled account of the flight of fugitive Templars to northern England and Scotland, and of their refusal to give up the quest they had undertaken centuries earlier in France and the Holy Land.

Like the Templars, the Scottish Masons refused to give up their campaign. And like the Templars, in the end they had to form a new organization to preserve their heritage.

As the Masons of London evolved into a modern organization, they abandoned such traditions as holding important events on the anniversary of the battle of Bannockburn. And they replaced ancient elements of the ritual with innovations like the Hiramic legend.

They did keep bits and pieces of the traditional workings, among them the old password. There is general agreement among scholars that today's Mason Word, which existed long before the formation of the Grand Lodge, is of Scottish origin. But no one remembers its meaning.

Even in eighteenth century London, such landmarks as these were becoming obscure remnants of the past. And the political climate of the time certainly kept the Scottish Masons from insisting that their real meaning be remembered and preserved.

So the lodge's ceremonies became even more obscure. As the Craft repaired the schism that had torn it apart, the ritual became literally a collection of symbols chosen by a committee. Much of it was still driven by the spirit it had received from the original Grail story, but the veiled history it once contained was lost. That history now survives only in the words of the York Legend and in the ritual of the Royal Order.

Before we leave that history behind, there is one last question to consider. We know why the French nobles of the twelfth century commissioned Chretien's poem in the first place, but we have yet to see if it succeed in its original purpose. We still haven't asked whether the Templars actually found the sacred relics they were seeking in the Holy Land.

They may have. Or at least they may have found what they believed were sacred relics. According to contemporary accounts, the True Cross – known in Scotland as the Holy Rood – turned up in Christian hands soon after the First Crusade. It was lost again during a battle at the Horns of Hattin in 1187, a disastrous defeat in which Templars were beheaded as soon as Saladin captured them. There are also persistent rumors that the Templars found and protected Christ's burial shroud. Those who believe this story claim the Templar's shroud is the one which now resides in the Italian town of Turin.

But physical relics, like Masonic symbols, have no meaning by themselves. They are merely icons that call our attention to a path leading to the spiritual insight for which we are all searching.

When Chretien and the Templars created the original ritual, they intended it to serve as the first step in a spiritual quest. This was – and still is – its true purpose.

When today's initiate enters the Masonic lodge for the first time, he encounters many symbols the Templar initiate of eight centuries ago would have seen. They teach the same lessons and point the way to the same goals. If the initiate studies them diligently, they will lead him on the same spiritual quest taken by the young Perceval. And even if the modern initiate's link with his Fraternity's past has been broken, he can still pursue the quest. After all, the quest has always been the thing of value that lies at the heart of the enterprise.

In a world where symbolism is no longer as important as it once was, it is good that the story of the Grail had survived in so many versions. And it is good that there is still a slender thread extending from the present to the twelfth century, a thread which those who are interested can follow until they eventually find the first Masonic ritual.

The precise nature of the original ritual can no longer be recovered. Too much has happened to it over the years for us to put the pieces back together. Though in a way it isn't the ritual that's important.

Today's Masons can compare their modern ritual with Chretien's work and see where the modern symbols came from. And anyone who has never seen a copy of the Masonic ritual or attended a meeting can look at the history of Chretien and the Templars and see where it all started.

The Masonic lodge, after all, is merely carrying on the quest Chretien and the Templars began all those centuries ago. And when dealing with a quest, it is always the journey that matters.

-end-

Bibliography

ANDERSON, JAMES, *Anderson's Constitutions of 1738*. Facsimile with commentary by Lewis Edwards and W.J.Hughan. Bloomington, Illinois: The Masonic Book Club, 1978.

Cannon, John and Griffiths, Ralph, *The Oxford Illustrated History of the British Monarchy*. Oxford: Oxford University Press, 1992.

Clark, F.R., "The Formation of the Grand Lodge of the Antients." *Transactions of the Lodge Quatuor Coronati*, vol. 79, 1966.

Denslow, William R. (forward by Harry S. Truman), *10,000 Famous Freemasons*. Richmond, Virginia: Macoy, 1957.

Durant, Will, *The Reformation*. New York: Simon and Schuster, 1957.

Franklin, Fay (ed), *History's Timeline*. New York: Crescent Books, 1981.

Godwin, Malcolm, *The Holy Grail: Its Origins, Secrets and Meaning Revealed*. London: Labyrinth, 1994.

"The Grand Lodge at York." *Transactions of the Lodge Quatuor Coronati*, vol 2, 1889.

Guignebert, Charles (Richmond, F.G., trans), *A Short History of the French People*. New York: The Macmillan Company, 1930. Vol 1.

BIBLIOGRAPHY

Holmes, Urban T. Jr. and Klenke, Sister M. Amelia, O.P., *Chretien, Troyes and the Grail*. Chapel Hill: The University of North Carolina Press, 1959.

Hamill, John, *The Craft - A History of English Freemasonry*. Wellingborough, England: Crucible, 1986.

Hughan, William James. "The York Grand Lodge - A Brief Sketch." *Transactions of the Lodge Quatuor Coronati*, vol 13, 1900.

Howarth, Stephen, *The Knights Templar*. New York: Antheneum, 1982.

Jones, Gwyn and Jones, Thomas (trans), *The Mabinogion*. Cambridge: Phoenix, 1996.

Kelly, Douglas (ed), *The Romances of Chretien de Troyes - A Symposium*. Lexington, Kentucky: French Forum, Publishers, 1985.

Kibler, William W. and Carroll, Carleton W. (trans), *Chretien de Troyes, Arthurian Romances*. London: Penguin Books, 1991.

Knoop, Douglas and Jones, G.P., *The Genesis of Freemasonry*. London: Quatuor Coronati Correspondence Circle, 1978.

Lennhoff, Eugen, *The Freemasons*. London: A Lewis Ltd, 1978.

Lindsay, Robert Strathern, *The Royal Order of Scotland*. Coupar Angus, Perthshire: Wm. Culross & Son Ltd., 1972.

McKerracher, Archie, "Bruce's Secret Weapon." *The Scots Magazine*, June 1991.

McNair Scott, Ronald, *Robert the Bruce King of Scots*. Edinburgh: Canongate, 1995.

BIBLIOGRAPHY

Morgan, Kenneth O. (ed), *The Oxford Illustrated History of Britain*. Oxford: Oxford University Press, 1984.

Mure MacKenzie, Agnes, *The Scotland of Queen Mary and the Religious Wars 1513-1638*. London: Alexander Maclehose & Co, 1936.

Mure MacKenzie, Agnes, *Robert Bruce King of Scots*. Edinburgh: Oliver & Boyd, 1956.

Ness, J.A., *History of the Antient Mother Lodge of Scotland*. Kilwinning: Mother Kilwinning Lodge No. 0, 1979.

The Official Ritual — Heredom of Kilwinning and Rosy Cross. Edinburgh: Grand Lodge of the Royal Order of Scotland, 1980.

Pick, Fred L. and Knight, G. Norman (revised by Frederick Smyth), *The Freemason's Pocket Reference Book*. London: Frederick Muller, Ltd, 1983.

Pick, Fred L. and Knight, G. Norman (revised by Frederick Smyth), *The Pocket History of Freemasonry*. London: Frederick Muller, Ltd, 1991.

Pickens, Rupert T. (ed) and Kibler, William W. (trans), *Chretien de Troyes, The Story of the Grail (Li Contes del Graal), or Perceval*. New York: Garland Publishing, Inc., 1990.

Romier, Lucien (Rowse, A.L., trans), *A History of France*. New York: St. Martin's Press, 1966.

Sadler, Henry. "An Unrecorded Grand Lodge." *Transactions of the Lodge Quatuor Coronati*, vol 18, 1905.